Life Among the Puritans

Among the

Titles in The Way People Live series include:

Cowboys in the Old West
Games of Ancient Rome
Life Among the Great Plains Indians
Life Among the Ibo Women of Nigeria
Life Among the Indian Fighters
Life Among the Pirates
Life Among the Puritans
Life Among the Samurai
Life Among the Vikings
Life During the Black Death
Life During the Crusades
Life During the French Revolution
Life During the Gold Rush
Life During the Great Depression
Life During the Middle Ages
Life During the Renaissance
Life During the Russian Revolution
Life During the Spanish Inquisition
Life in a Japanese American Internment
   Camp
Life in a Medieval Castle
Life in America During the 1960s
Life in a Nazi Concentration Camp
Life in an Amish Community
Life in Ancient Athens
Life in Ancient China
Life in Ancient Egypt
Life in Ancient Greece
Life in Ancient Rome
Life in a Medieval Monastery

Life in a Wild West Show
Life in Berlin
Life in Charles Dickens's England
Life in Communist Russia
Life in Genghis Khan's Mongolia
Life in Moscow
Life in the Amazon Rain Forest
Life in the American Colonies
Life in the Elizabethan Theater
Life in the Hitler Youth
Life in the North During the Civil War
Life in the South During the Civil War
Life in the Warsaw Ghetto
Life in Tokyo
Life in War-Torn Bosnia
Life of a Medieval Knight
Life of a Nazi Soldier
Life of a Roman Slave
Life of a Roman Soldier
Life of a Slave on a Southern Plantation
Life on Alcatraz
Life on a Medieval Pilgrimage
Life on an African Slave Ship
Life on an Everest Expedition
Life on Ellis Island
Life on the American Frontier
Life on the Oregon Trail
Life on the Pony Express
Life on the Underground Railroad
Life Under the Jim Crow Laws

THE WAY PEOPLE LIVE

Life Among the Puritans

by
Louise Chipley Slavicek

Lucent Books, P.O. Box 289011, San Diego, CA 92198-9011

For my father, George W. Chipley

Library of Congress Cataloging-in-Publication Data

Slavicek, Louise Chipley, 1956–
    Life among the Puritans / by Louise Chipley Slavicek
        p. cm. — (The way people live)
Includes bibliographical references and index.
    ISBN 1-56006-869-8 (alk. paper)
    1. Puritans—New England—Social life and customs—Juvenile literature. 2.
Puritans—New England—Social conditions—Juvenile literature. 3. New
England—Social life and customs—To 1775—Juvenile literature. 4. New
England—Social conditions—17th century—Juvenile literature. [1. Puritans. 2.
New England—Social life and customs—To 1775.] I. Title. II. Series.
    F757 .S55 2001
    974'.02—dc21

                                                              00-012664

Contents

FOREWORD
Discovering the Humanity in Us All   6

INTRODUCTION
Coming to a New World   8

CHAPTER ONE
Creating a New Society   12

CHAPTER TWO
Religion and the Supernatural   24

CHAPTER THREE
Working   38

CHAPTER FOUR
At Home   52

CHAPTER FIVE
Growing up Puritan   67

CHAPTER SIX
Health and Medicine   79

EPILOGUE
The Puritan Legacy   92

Notes   95
For Further Reading   99
Works Consulted   100
Index   103
Picture Credits   107
About the Author   108

Discovering the Humanity in Us All

Books in The Way People Live series focus on groups of people in a wide variety of circumstances, settings, and time periods. Some books focus on different cultural groups, others, on people in a particular historical time period, while others cover people involved in a specific event. Each book emphasizes the daily routines, personal and historical struggles, and achievements of people from all walks of life.

To really understand any culture, it is necessary to strip the mind of the common notions we hold about groups of people. These stereotypes are the archenemies of learning. It does not even matter whether the stereotypes are positive or negative; they are confining and tight. Removing them is a challenge that's not easily met, as anyone who has ever tried it will admit. Ideas that do not fit into the templates we create are unwelcome visitors—ones we would prefer remain quietly in a corner or forgotten room.

The cowboy of the Old West is a good example of such confining roles. The cowboy was courageous, yet soft-spoken. His time (it is always a he, in our template) was spent alternatively saving a rancher's daughter from certain death on a runaway stagecoach, or shooting it out with rustlers. At times, of course, he was likely to get a little crazy in town after a trail drive, but for the most part, he was the epitome of inner strength. It is disconcerting to find out that the cowboy is human, even a bit childish. Can it really be true that cowboys would line up to help the cook on the trail drive grind coffee, just hoping he would give them a little stick of peppermint candy that came with the coffee shipment? The idea of tough cowboys vying with one another to help "Coosie" (as they called their cooks) for a bit of candy seems silly and out of place.

So is the vision of Eskimos playing video games and watching MTV, living in prefab housing in the Arctic. It just does not fit with what "Eskimo" means. We are far more comfortable with snow igloos and whale blubber, harpoons and kayaks.

Although the cultures dealt with in Lucent's The Way People Live series are often historically and socially well known, the emphasis is on the personal aspects of life. Groups of people, while unquestionably affected by their politics and their governmental structures, are more than those institutions. How do people in a particular time and place educate their children? What do they eat? And how do they build their houses? What kinds of work do they do? What kinds of games do they enjoy? The answers to these questions bring these cultures to life. People's lives are revealed in the particulars and only by knowing the particulars can we understand these cultures' will to survive and their moments of weakness and greatness.

This is not to say that understanding politics does not help to understand a culture. There is no question that the Warsaw ghetto, for example, was a culture that was brought about by the politics and social ideas of Adolf

Hitler and the Third Reich. But the Jews who were crowded together in the ghetto cannot be understood by the Reich's politics. Their life was a day-to-day battle for existence, and the creativity and methods they used to prolong their lives is a vital story of human perseverance that would be denied by focusing only on the institutions of Hitler's Germany. Knowing that children as young as five or six outwitted Nazi guards on a daily basis, that Jewish policemen helped the Germans control the ghetto, that children attended secret schools in the ghetto and even earned diplomas—these are the things that reveal the fabric of life, that can inspire, intrigue, and amaze.

Books in The Way People Live series allow both the casual reader and the student to see humans as victims, heroes, and onlookers. And although humans act in ways that can fill us with feelings of sorrow and revulsion, it is important to remember that "hero," "predator," and "victim" are dangerous terms. Heaping undue pity or praise on people reduces them to objects, and strips them of their humanity.

Seeing the Jews of Warsaw only as victims is to deny their humanity. Seeing them only as they appear in surviving photos, staring at the camera with infinite sadness, is limiting, both to them and to those who want to understand them. To an object of pity, the only appropriate response becomes "Those poor creatures!" and that reduces both the quality of their struggle and the depth of their despair. No one is served by such two-dimensional views of people and their cultures.

With this in mind, The Way People Live series strives to flesh out the traditional, two-dimensional views of people in various cultures and historical circumstances. Using a wide variety of primary quotations—the words not only of the politicians and government leaders, but of the real people whose lives are being examined—each book in the series attempts to show an honest and complete picture of a culture removed from our own by time or space.

By examining cultures in this way, the reader will notice not only the glaring differences from his or her own culture, but also will be struck by the similarities. For indeed, people share common needs—warmth, good company, stability, and affirmation from others. Ultimately, seeing how people really live, or have lived, can only enrich our understanding of ourselves.

Coming to a New World

In September 1620, an aged sailing ship named the *Mayflower* set out from England bound for the New World. On board was a small but determined band of men, women, and children known today as the Pilgrims. After a perilous, two-month voyage, the Pilgrims finally landed at Plymouth, in the region of North America called New England. There they imme-

diately started work on the task that had brought them three thousand miles from their homeland. They began to build a new society, a society founded on their Puritan ideals. Puritanism was a religious movement that stressed personal faith and living according to scriptural standards over church ritual, and the individual congregation over bishops and other church officials.

The Mayflower *transported the Pilgrims from England to the New World in September 1620.*

A decade after the Pilgrims stepped ashore at Plymouth, a larger and better-financed group of Puritans departed the British Isles for New England under the leadership of John Winthrop. The fleet made landfall just north of Plymouth, near the site of present-day Boston. Like the Pilgrims before them, the founders of the new Massachusetts Bay Colony came to America in hopes of establishing an entire society based on their Puritan principles. Over the course of the seventeenth century, thousands more English Puritans would abandon their homeland to join their fellow believers in creating a refuge in the New England wilderness for what they viewed as the one true faith.

The Reformation

The story of the New England Puritans began a century before the *Mayflower* set sail, when the German monk Martin Luther sparked the Reformation by protesting what he viewed as corruption within the Catholic Church. Led by the pope in Rome, the Catholic Church had monopolized religious life in Europe for centuries. But with the advent of Luther and other reformers like John Calvin of France, Catholicism began to lose its hold over western Christianity. In time, the followers of these reformers, who were called Protestants, established separate Christian denominations of their own.

In 1534 the Reformation reached England when King Henry VIII created the Church of England, explicitly removing English Catholics from the pope's authority. The English monarch, not the pope, was the head of the new English or Anglican Communion. However, Henry's disagreement with the Catholic Church was founded on politics rather than religion; though in his struggle for control he dramatically altered the hierarchy of the church, he left its teachings nearly unchanged.

A statue in Worms Park, Germany, depicts Martin Luther, who instigated the Reformation by denouncing the corruption he saw within the Catholic Church.

The Development of Puritanism

Some English people were dissatisified with the course that the Reformation had taken in their country. They believed that it had not gone far enough. These disgruntled Protestants, who came to be known as Puritans, hoped to "purify" the Church of England of all practices which they considered to be "popish." In opposition to the wishes of both church and government officials in England, the Puritans sought to give more power to individual congregations, bar the royal government from interfering with the church, and place more emphasis on the Scriptures and less on ritual in worship. The most radical wing of the Puritan movement, the Separatists, wanted to break away entirely from the Anglican Communion and establish their own church. The Pilgrims belonged to this faction.

All Puritans followed the religious teachings of John Calvin. Like Calvin, they stressed the absolute power of God and the absolute sinfulness of humankind. They also adopted Calvin's concept of predestination. Predestination is the belief that from the beginning of time, God has predestined some people for salvation and eternal life and others for eternal damnation. In the course of his life on earth, no believer can know with absolute certainty whether he is among the saved, or "Elect." Nor can he do anything whatsoever to win his salva-

tion. Although the Puritans believed that good actions could not earn them eternal life, they still emphasized the importance of upright behavior as a sign that a believer was probably one of the Elect.

The Emigrants

Not everyone who settled in New England during the course of the seventeenth century was a Puritan. Yet the vast majority were. Religious concerns seem to have played a central role in convincing most of the Puritan colonists to leave England. They sought both to escape religious persecution at home and to help their Puritan brothers and sisters build a godly new society in America.

Many Puritans left England for America in order to escape religious persecution.

Aside from their Puritan beliefs, the emigrants shared a number of other common traits. Nearly all of them came to New England as part of a family group, in contrast to the band of primarily young, unattached males who settled Virginia, the first British colony in America. A majority of the emigrants were members of England's middle class; most had earned comfortable livings in the mother country as craftsmen or farmers. Nonetheless, a sizable minority of the Puritan colonists, including John Winthrop, belonged to their homeland's wealthy upper class. Also in contrast to Virginia's early settlers, almost all of the New England settlers had some education; a select few, like Winthrop, had attended college.

The Puritans Spread Out

At first, Puritan New England consisted of a narrow band of settlements along the Massachusetts coast. But as more and more settlers poured into New England, Puritan expansion into other parts of the region became inevitable. The immigrants began spreading out from the Plymouth and Massachusetts Bay Colonies to the present-day states of Connecticut and Rhode Island in 1636, New Hampshire in 1638, and Maine in 1652.

Until the final years of the seventeenth century, Puritan ideas about government, society, family, and education predominated throughout the New England colonies. The Puritans also managed to maintain a stranglehold on the region's religious life during most of the 1600s. Only in tiny Rhode Island was Puritanism forced to compete with other denominations or sects during the early colonial period. For nearly a century after the Pilgrims set sail for America, Puritan control over New England culture and society would remain virtually unchallenged.

Creating a New Society

While still at sea, John Winthrop preached a famous sermon explaining the Puritan mission to America: "We must consider that we shall be as a city upon a hill, the eyes of all people are upon us,"[1] Winthrop proclaimed. Puritan New England was to be a model for the world to follow, a beacon of holiness in a dark and sinful world.

Winthrop went on to outline the Puritans' goals for their "city upon a hill." First, every citizen would put the good of the whole above his or her own desires. We "must bear one another's burdens," he preached, "always having before our eyes our . . . community in the work." Second, the "city" would be a God-fearing society. If the settlers obeyed God's laws, Winthrop declared, God will "bless us in the land whither we go." But if "we will not obey," he warned, "we shall surely perish." Last, each colonist would know and accept his or her place in the social order. God had designed human society as a hierarchy, the Puritans taught, with the rich and educated at the top, and the poor at the bottom. God "hath so disposed of the condition of mankind," explained Winthrop, "as in all times some must be rich, some poor, some high . . . in power and dignity, others mean and in subjection."[2]

The ideas that Winthrop outlined—the Puritans' sense of community, their emphasis on living morally, and their belief that social inequality was ordained by God—formed the foundation upon which the settlers built their new society. These concepts shaped the way Puritans set up their towns, distributed their land, designed their government and legal system, and treated their poor.

Creating Towns

In the 1600s, the British Crown granted charters conveying proprietary rights to large tracts of land to certain groups or individuals in America. These broad agreements permitted the various colonies to govern themselves with little interference from the king, an arrange-

John Winthrop outlined the ideas that became the foundation of Puritan society.

This replica of a Puritan village reflects the Puritan belief in a tightly knit community.

ment which suited New England's Puritan settlers perfectly. If the Puritans hoped to fulfill their dream of establishing a holy "city upon a hill," they could hardly allow the head of the Church of England to manage their affairs.

The Puritan founders of New England were determined to settle the land granted to them by the Crown in their own way. Individuals were forbidden from applying to their colonial government for land. Requests for land on which to build towns had to be made by groups of families.

The Puritan officials' insistence that New England be settled by groups of families, rather than by individuals, was rooted in their communal ideal. If the Puritan settlers were "to be knit together as one,"[3] as Winthrop put it, they must reside near one another. Only by living, worshiping, and working side by side in compact towns could the Puritans build the tightly knit communities they thought God favored.

The grants of land allotted to a particular New England town varied in size, with most

being about one hundred square miles. This figure was far from generous, considering the tremendous amount of available land. Yet the Puritan officials knew what they were doing. People who lived near one another would be able to scrutinize their neighbors' behavior, they reasoned. Today, most Americans cherish their privacy, viewing it as a basic personal right. But the Puritans saw privacy as a luxury they could ill afford. And little wonder, since they believed that wicked behavior by just one townsperson might cause God to punish the entire community.

Distributing Land

After a group of families received a town grant, the men who had applied for it distributed the land among the different households. They presented a home lot near the town center to every head of a household. The size of the lots varied; some people got more land than others.

The size of a family's lot was most often determined by its members' economic standing back in England. As Winthrop made clear in his shipboard sermon, social and economic equality were not Puritan goals. Some people would always be wealthier and more influential than others, the Puritans assumed, for that was God's plan for society. The proposal for land distribution drawn up by the founders of Andover, Massachusetts, was typical of those used

Settlers and Natives

When the Puritans arrived in New England, they found that the region was inhabited by several tribes of Native Americans, all members of the Algonquian family. Historians estimate that no more than fifteen thousand Native Americans lived in New England when the Pilgrims arrived in 1620. On the eve of the Puritan migration, disease epidemics introduced by European explorers and fishermen had reduced the Algonquian population by as much as 40 percent.

Chief Metacomet, or King Philip, leader of the alliance of tribes that fought against the Puritans in 1675.

At first, relations between the Puritans and the Native Americans were amicable. Local tribes taught the colonists important survival skills, such as how to plant corn and other New World plants and where to hunt. Much of New England was not held by a particular tribe, and most Native Americans had no objections to having the settlers farm the unclaimed lands. When the Puritans wanted territory held by a tribe, they paid for it in goods the Native Americans wanted like cloth, metalware, and tools.

As New England's white population grew, however, tensions developed between the Puritans and the Native Americans. As the settlers pushed deeper inland, more and more native hunting grounds were lost and some tribes began to feel squeezed. Many Native Americans also resented Puritan efforts to convert them to their religion and make them adhere to colonial laws. In 1675 war broke out between the Puritans and an alliance of disgruntled tribes led by Chief Metacomet, or King Philip, as he was known to the colonists. Metacomet was killed after a year of fighting and many of his followers were captured and sold into slavery in the British West Indies.

in countless New England towns. In their plan, Andover's founders resolved to "give every Inhabitant whome they received as a Townsman an house lott proportionable to his estate [rank in society]."[4]

Although the size of the home lots in a town varied, all were at least large enough to include a "kitchen" garden for growing vegetables like turnips and onions, and a small orchard for apple or other fruit trees. Each family, in addition to a home lot, received a portion of the fields, meadows, and forests surrounding the town center. Once again, the size of a family's plot was tied to its social and economic rank. People at the top of the social hierarchy got the biggest plots, as well as those most conveniently located in relation to the town center.

Puritan landowners were free to pass their land on to their heirs as they saw fit. They could also sell their property to someone from outside the town, but only after their neighbors decided that the would-be owner was fit to join the community. This they accomplished by grilling the prospective buyer about his religious beliefs and moral behavior. When the town of Dedham, Massachusetts, was settled in 1636, its founders set down in writing their determination that all newcomers share their Puritan beliefs: "We shall by all means labor to keep off from us all such as are contrary minded, and receive only such unto us as may be probably one heart with us."[5]

Laying Out the Town

Most towns in Puritan New England shared the same basic design. In many ways, they looked like the villages the settlers had left behind in England. As was true in the majority of English villages, the townspeoples' houses were clustered around a central common—a communal grazing spot for cattle, sheep, and other live-

The Puritans constructed gristmills to grind grain into flour.

stock. Although New Englanders liked to refer to their common as the "green," this area was more likely to be brown. The grazing animals trampled its grass, leaving the town common a muddy eyesore. Near the green, or in some other prominent spot in town, stood the meetinghouse, which was used as both a church and a town hall. No New England town could exist without a meetinghouse, and building one was usually a town's first order of business. In time, the center of the town might also contain a schoolhouse, a few shops, a tavern, and perhaps a garrison house or two for defense against attacks by Native Americans.

Within a few years of initial settlement, most New England towns also had a gristmill for grinding grain from the colonists' fields into flour. Typically, the entire community worked together to construct the mill. Mills were situated near a river or stream, which the builders dammed to create a millpond. Water from the millpond powered the huge waterwheel that turned the grindstone.

Governing the Towns

After handing out home lots, woodlots, and fields, and putting aside land for a green and a meetinghouse, the town's founders were ready to tackle their next job: creating a local government. By far the most important government in the day-to-day lives of the Puritans was their town government. Once a town's founders had obtained a land grant from their colony's central government, they and their town enjoyed a great deal of independence. Towns ran their own elections, collected their own taxes, and decided how to spend their revenues. Towns were also responsible for organizing and training their own citizen armies, called militias. (There were no colonywide armies in British America.)

In most towns, the founders composed a covenant, or contract, to be signed by all heads of households as the first step in creating their government. The covenants mirrored the vision of community emphasized by Winthrop. Most included a statement underscoring the founders' commitment to promoting peace and cooperation among the townspeople.

Town Meetings

The concern for a closely knit community apparent in the Puritans' town covenants was also reflected in the way they ran their local governments. Towns held yearly meetings to choose officials including clerks (record keepers), tax collectors, fence viewers (who made sure that fences were properly placed and maintained), cattle catchers, and hog reeves (who rounded up stray pigs). The chief town officials were the selectmen. Among the selectmen's duties were overseeing the work of lesser officials, admitting new inhabitants, ensuring that roads and bridges were maintained, and settling disputes among townspeople. They formally met nearly every month to hear complaints and conduct their regular business.

In hopes of encouraging a sense of unity among the townspeople, the selectmen urged all adult male citizens to attend town meetings. In many communities, a man could actually be punished for missing a meeting. In Dorchester, Massachusetts, for example, any townsman who failed to show up at a town meeting without a good excuse was fined sixpence.

Even those townsmen who could not vote were supposed to be present at the meetings. All the New England colonies stipulated that voters must be landholders, a requirement that most settlers had no trouble fulfilling. But many New England towns put an additional restriction on voting. In numerous towns, only "church members" were permitted to vote. Being a church member meant more to the Puritans than showing up at the meetinghouse on Sundays. Indeed, in many Puritan meetinghouses, the majority of the congregation were not church members, athough they still considered themselves to be devout Christians. Church members had to prove to their minister that they had personally experienced God's presence in their lives or heard his voice. Although the Puritan clergy taught that no believer could know with absolute certainty whether he or she had been selected by God for eternal life, church members were generally assumed to be among the saved, or Elect. Whether church members or not, women were strictly barred from voting in town meetings and colonywide elections. In Puritan New England, politics was for men only.

Leaders and Followers

The Puritans' concern for an orderly society, as much as their desire for a closely knit one, shaped the way they ran their town governments. Year after year, voters entrusted their community's most prominent members with the top political posts. Accustomed to giving their political support to upper-class men back in England, the Puritans naturally assumed that high social status and the ability to govern went hand in hand. Poor men were generally thought to lack the self-confidence and dignity necessary to exert authority over others. If lower-class men were elected to political office, the Reverend John Bulkley warned, all order in society would be overturned, and the government would "sink in the mire of popular confusion."[6]

Government officials were to be treated with respect at all times. Citizens should "honour, submit to, and obey those whom God hath set over us,"[7] declared the founders of Dedham in their town covenant. "Guidance belongs to leaders, Obedience to their followers, whose wisdom it is to obey rather than dispute the commands of their Superiors,"[8] the Reverend William Hubbard reminded the people of Massachusetts in an election day sermon in 1676. Anyone who slighted a government official could expect to be punished, ministers warned. Thus in 1649, the Reverend Samuel Newman of Plymouth was hauled into court for preaching a sermon in which he allegedly slandered the colony's magistrates.

Constables and Watchmen

One of the most important governmental posts in any New England town was that of constable, who was like a modern-day policeman. The constable's central duties were described in a typical Massachusetts law:

The Puritans' preoccupation with social status was reflected in the forms of address they used. Men near the top of the social scale were addressed as "Mr." or "Master" and their wives as "Mrs." or "Mistress." A young girl from an upper-class family was also called "Mrs.," even though she was unmarried. Thus the Reverend Cotton Mather wrote in his diary of a certain "Mrs. Sarah Gerrish, a very beautiful and ingenious damsel of seven years of age."

Any man who was not a member of the gentry—in other words, someone who was not a minister, high government official, or wealthy landowner or merchant—was addressed as "Goodman." His wife was known as "Goodwife," which was sometimes shortened to "Goody."

Every constable . . . hath, by virtue of his office, full power to make, signe, & put forth pursuits, or hues & cries, after murderers, manslayers, peace breakers, theeves, robbers, burglarers . . . also to apprehend without warrant such as are over taken with drinke, swearing, breaking ye Sabbath, lying, vagrant persons . . . or any other [who] shall break our lawes.[9]

Constables worked only during daytime hours. After dark, night watchmen patrolled the streets of New England's towns, looking for "night walkers" (curfew breakers) and other miscreants. In Boston, the town watchmen were specifically instructed to suppress any "disturbances" such as "danceing, drinckeing, Singinge vainlie [that is, singing popular songs instead of hymns], &c."[10] Watchmen were also

Puritan townspeople worked together to build meetinghouses, schools, and other community structures.

supposed to be on the lookout for any evidence of fire or of an Indian attack. To sound the alarm, watchmen rang a bell or twirled a noise-making device called a rattle.

The Common Good

In every town in Puritan New England, people were expected to devote a certain amount of time to collective tasks. Townspeople worked together to build roads and bridges; erect meetinghouses, schools, and gristmills and repair communal fences. Firefighting was another communal duty. In most towns, every homeowner was required by law to keep a fire bucket outside his home. Each head of a household was expected to grab the bucket and come running if a fire alarm was sounded anywhere in town. At the site of the fire, the townsmen formed a bucket brigade, in which buckets of water from the nearest pond or stream were passed up a line and tossed on the fire, then passed back down a second line to be refilled.

The Puritans also put their communal ideal into practice in their treatment of their colonies' least fortunate members. Town officials organized relief for victims of floods or fires and assumed responsibility for their community's orphans, physically or mentally disabled citizens, and anyone whom they believed to be among the "worthy poor." By the term "worthy poor," the Puritans meant those who could not support themselves or their family through no fault of their own. Puritan officials, however, had no sympathy for those colonists they considered to be the "idle poor"—people who, although capable of supporting themselves or their dependents, failed to do so.[11] In 1682 the selectmen of Boston resolved to withhold all public assistance from "persons & Families [who] misspend their time, in idleness & tipplings with great neglect of their callings and suffer ye Children shamefully to spend their time in ye Streets."[12]

"Idlers" and "vagrants" were sometimes threatened with expulsion from a colony unless they found employment. Robert Pinion of Plymouth, for instance, was arrested as a vagrant in 1667, publicly whipped, and ordered to depart the colony immediately. A few years later, William Batt, having resisted every attempt by the Boston selectmen to put him to work, was evicted from New England altogether and shipped off to the West Indies.

Crime, Puritan Style

Every society has a different idea of what constitutes a crime. In Puritan New England, a remarkable range of behaviors was considered criminal, including meddling, scolding, gossiping, eavesdropping, cursing, sleeping during church services, lying, and neglecting your work. Countless seventeenth-century New Englanders came before the courts each year as complainants, defendants, or witnesses. The Puritans' judicial system was designed to encourage people, forcibly if necessary, to live according to biblical standards. This was a crucially important task since the Puritans believed that God would punish their entire society for any uncorrected departures from proper behavior.

Firefighting

Little wonder the Puritans made firefighting a communal responsibility, for fire posed a constant danger in their closely settled towns. The difficulties of controlling fires were enormous in colonial New England. There was always a good chance that a fire would spread from its original source to nearby houses or buildings, most of which were constructed from wood and filled with wooden furniture and household goods of equally flammable materials.

New England's most densely populated town, Boston, was especially vulnerable to the ravages of fire. In 1678, after a fire destroyed nearly fifty buildings in Boston, the town purchased New England's first fire engine. It was a simple device featuring a tub for holding water, a hand-operated pump, and a snakelike nozzle. The wooden engine was clumsy to use and to transport—it had no wheels and had to be carried to the scene of the fire. Even after the town acquired a fire engine, firefighting remained a communal effort in Boston, since bucket brigades were required to fill the machine's large holding tub with water.

Although church and government were not officially joined in Puritan New England, ministers and magistrates cooperated closely in the day-to-day running of the "city upon a hill." Colonial governments passed laws designed to enforce uniformity in upholding the Puritan faith. Thus, New Englanders could be severely punished by state officials for purely religious transgressions such as heresy (expressing unorthodox religious opinions) or blasphemy (speaking irreverently of God). In Massachusetts, the punishment for blasphemy was a six-month prison sentence, a public whipping, and either sitting on the gallows with a rope around your neck or having your tongue bored through with a red-hot iron. Idolatry (the worship of idols) was actually punishable by death in some Puritan colonies, although no New Englander was ever convicted of the crime.

Town and colonial governments also strictly enforced laws regarding the Sabbath. Puritan officials designated the twenty-four hours from sunset Saturday to sunset Sunday as a time of rest and religious contemplation. When people were not in church, they were supposed to be at home, quietly reading the Bible or other religious books or praying. Every other sort of activity was prohibited on the Sabbath, including playing, fishing, and all work. The Puritans even passed regulations against walking too fast or laughing too loudly on Sundays.

Public displays of affection on the Sabbath were also prohibited. In Boston, a Captain Kemble, who had just returned home after three years at sea, was hauled before the courts for "lewd and unseemly behavior"[13] when he kissed his wife on his front doorstep on the Sabbath.

The strictly enforced Sabbath was designated as a time of rest and religious contemplation.

Puritans who broke the law were sometimes forced to sit or stand in the stocks or pillories for hours.

Lawyers and Judges

Most people in Puritan New England were obliged to represent themselves in court. Few lawyers set up practices in New England during the seventeenth century, for English Puritans had a reputation for distrusting lawyers. Lawyers were also viewed with suspicion in the New World colonies the Puritans established.

New Englanders were strongly encouraged by both their town and colonial governments to settle disputes without the assistance of paid attorneys. Indeed, being represented by a paid lawyer was actually illegal in Massachusetts for a period of several years during the 1640s. Of the handful of New Englanders who were able to make a living through practicing law, the ma-

jority had learned their profession by acting as assistants to established lawyers. Few held an advanced degree. Even most judges had no formal training in the law.

Punishing the Ungodly

Puritan magistrates believed that criminals should feel shame for their acts, and the punishments they meted out reflected this attitude. Being made to sit or stand for extended periods in the stocks or pillories was an especially popular means of shaming wrongdoers. Stocks and pillories were wooden devices with openings for securing a person's legs, arms, or head. They were located on the common, or some other central spot in town. Being put in the stocks or the pillory was uncomfortable as well as humiliating. Offenders were forced to remain motionless in the contraptions for as long as six hours at a time while passersby taunted them and pelted them with dirt or rotten fruit and vegetables. The first person to be placed in the stocks in Boston was a carpenter by the name of Edward Palmer. Ironically, Palmer's crime was overcharging the town for his work in constructing the stocks.

In addition to stocks and pillories, many New England towns used "ducking chairs" to humiliate criminals. A ducking chair consisted of a simple wooden chair attached to a long beam. The wrongdoer was secured to the chair by an iron band, then plunged into a river or stream, with the number of duckings set by the court. Ducking was typically used to punish women accused of "scolding" (nagging or quarreling). In 1672 the Massachusetts General Court ordered that anyone accused of scolding should be either gagged or "set in a ducking-stool and dipped over head and ears three times."[14]

Puritan judges had many ingenious ways to shame lawbreakers. Some offenders were ordered to stand at the door of the meetinghouse holding a sign explaining their crime. Others were made to pin onto their clothing a large cloth letter symbolizing the crime they had committed. For instance, a Boston man accused of repeated drunkenness was sentenced to wear a red *D* on his clothing for one year, while Katherine Ainis of Plymouth was commanded to wear a large *B* "sewed to her upper garments," apparently for the crime of "blabbing" (gossiping).[15]

For more serious offenses such as theft or assault, offenders were frequently sentenced to whippings, with the number of lashes dependent on the severity of the crime. In Massachusetts, burglars were punished by having the letter *B* branded on their forehead with a hot iron. Harsh physical punishments like whipping or branding were performed in full view of the townspeople, for Puritan magistrates believed that the most effective deterrent to crime was the public infliction of punishment.

Executions

The crime of murder was punishable by death, usually by hanging. Advertised weeks in advance, executions were major public events in Puritan New England. Huge crowds attended executions—as many as five thousand people attended one hanging in Boston. Drums were played, ministers delivered sermons, and lurid pamphlets describing the criminal and his crime were hastily printed up and sold. Tearful, last-minute confessions by the condemned criminal added to the drama of the event. Joseph Quason, a Native American convicted of murdering another Native American, delivered a particularly stirring speech from the scaffold before he was executed. When an emotional Quason admonished the crowd to learn from his example and renounce wickedness, his spellbound listeners were moved "almost beyond Example,"[16] noted one eyewitness.

One of the most publicized hangings in the history of Boston took place several years later when seven pirates were executed off the city's shore. Gallows were erected between the high- and low-water marks of a small point of land. The diarist Samuel Sewall described the event in his journal:

> When I came to see how the River was cover'd with People, I was amazed: Some say there were 100 Boats. 150 Boats and Canoes, saith Cousin Moodey. . . .When the scaffold was hoisted to a due height, the seven Malefactors went up: Mr. [Cotton]

Advertised weeks in advance, Puritan public executions were witnessed by large crowds.

Mather [one of the leading Puritan clergymen of the day] pray'd for them standing upon the Boat. . . . When the scaffold was let to sink, there was such a Screech of the Women that my wife heard it sitting in our Entry next to the Orchard, and was much surprised at it; yet the wind was sou-west. Our house is a full mile from the place.[17]

Few people were imprisoned for crimes in Puritan New England. Throughout the seventeenth century, the cost of constructing and maintaining prisons was simply too burdensome for most towns to handle. When town officials had to hold a suspect in custody, the constable typically placed the accused person in some type of makeshift jail, such as a room in a tavern.

Religion and the Supernatural

Religion was ever present in the lives of the Puritans. The location of the meetinghouse at the center of town was symbolic of the place of the church in Puritan society. A desire to scrutinize one another's behavior was one reason why the Puritans built their homes close together around their town center. An equally important reason was so that every townsperson would live within walking distance of the meetinghouse.

The Meetinghouse

Most seventeenth-century New England meetinghouses were constructed according to the same basic design. The typical meetinghouse was a simple, square, one-room building. It did not have a steeple or bell tower, which the Puritans regarded as "popish." Also reflecting the Puritans' disdain for what they considered to be the "Catholic pomp" of the Anglican churches, their meetinghouses omitted stained-glass windows, statues, or ornaments of any sort. The focal point of the entire building was a plain wood pulpit.

According to the Puritans, worshipers were not meant to be comfortable in church. A little suffering was good for the soul, they believed. Hard, backless, wooden benches provided the congregation's seating. Constructed without fireplaces, meetinghouses

In contrast to the ornate design of the Catholic Church, the Puritan meetinghouse was designed to be plain and simple.

Preassigned seating was strictly enforced at mandatory Puritan church services.

were cold and drafty throughout the long New England winters. Worshipers carried heated bricks or stones wrapped in blankets with them to church to serve as foot warmers. The family dog was often brought to church for the same purpose. Now and then, a dog would tire of lying quietly atop his master's or mistress's feet and begin chasing another dog up and down the aisles. Pandemonium reigned until the animals were collared by their flustered owners.

In their neverending quest to stay warm during the winter months, Puritan congregations were sometimes willing to sacrifice light for heat. In New Haven, Connecticut, town officials declared that "the Casements [windows] of the Meeting House may have the glass taken out and boards fitted in, that in the winter it may bee warme; and in the summer they may bee taken downe to let in the ayre."[18]

When New Englanders entered their meetinghouses on Sunday mornings, they headed straight for preassigned seats. Men and women sat on opposite sides of the meetinghouse. Girls and young boys stayed with their mothers, older boys sat—and sometimes stood—at the far back of the church or under the gallery (balcony). In Salem, it was decreed that all boys of the town "sitt upon ye three paire of stairs in ye meetinghouse."[19] Also relegated to the back of the church were the community's poorest members. The prize seats—the benches near the pulpit—were reserved for the town's most prominent citizens. Puritan congregations took their seating arrangements seriously. Worshipers who failed to stay in their assigned spots were fined stiffly.

Church Services

The main Puritan services were held on Sundays and attendance was mandatory. In most towns, people also flocked to the meetinghouse on Thursday evenings to hear a midweek sermon. Sunday services were timed by an hourglass kept on the pulpit. They lasted for up to three hours in the morning, and two hours in the afternoon. Congregations went home for a midday meal break between the A.M. and P.M. services.

Thomas Lechford, a Boston lawyer, described a typical Sabbath service, which opened

Puritans travel to a meetinghouse to observe a day of thanksgiving.

with the pastor delivering "a solemn prayer continuing about a quarter of an hour. The teacher [the assistant minister] then readeth and expoundeth a chapter [from the Bible], then a psalm is sung. . . . After that the pastor preacheth a sermon, and sometimes *ex tempore* exhorts [departs from his prepared speech to emphasize a point]. Then the teacher concludes with a prayer and blessing."[20] Once a month, special Holy Communion services were held at which the symbolic bread and wine of the Lord's Supper was offered to those in the congregation who had been certified by their minister as members of the church.

Puritan services did not include organ music or any other kind of instrumental music. Instrumental music distracted the churchgoer's attention from God, the Puritans believed. Congregations were permitted to sing psalms (poetic expressions of praise, prayer, and commemoration found in the Bible). However, there were no choir directors or hymnals in Puritan churches. Instead, a congregation member known as a "liner" called out a line from a psalm, and the rest of the worshipers repeated it in whatever tunes they wished, often with quite unmelodious results. One exasperated parson in Connecticut chided his flock for "sliding from one tune to another while singing or singing the same line in different tunes."[21]

In addition to attending church on Thursdays and Sundays, New Englanders were expected to drop their work and head for the meetinghouse whenever a "fast" or "thanksgiving" day was announced. Days of thanksgiving were called when the community enjoyed an especially good harvest or had been delivered from some trouble. Townspeople gathered at the meetinghouse to offer up prayers of thanks and the service was usually followed by a feast. The choice of a day in late November, celebrated as Thanksgiving Day in the United States, has its roots in this tradition.

Fast days were called whenever a community suffered a calamity such as severe weather or a disease epidemic. Townspeople fasted from sundown to sundown. They spent much of the day in church, repenting of their sins. The Puritans usually interpreted community disasters as results of their own shortcomings. They believed that they had failed God by being proud or greedy or lazy, and God had punished them.

By the same token, they believed that if the congregation was genuinely repentant and the fast day successful, they would be back in church again soon, this time for a day of thanksgiving to God for delivering them from their affliction. Indeed, in 1639 Puritans all over the Massachusetts Bay Colony attended fast day services when a drought threatened to destroy their crops. Soon afterward, a Puritan official reported that God sent "such [a] store of rain, and so seasonably as the corn revived and gave hope of a very plentiful harvest."[22]

The Puritans and Christmas

Although colonywide celebrations were held to give thanks for the drought-ending

Governor William Bradford (far right) cautions townspeople against celebrating Christmas, a holiday he did not believe should be observed.

rain of 1639, Puritans did not celebrate the familiar Christian holidays. They justified their refusal to permit Christmas festivities by observing that the Scriptures give no specific date for the birth of Jesus. Puritan leaders were convinced that the Catholic Church had arbitrarily chosen December 25 to coincide with the winter celebrations traditionally held by pagan sects. They suspected early churchmen of trying to win over the pagan groups by offering them a different festival to replace their traditional winter partying.

Puritans were expected to work as usual on December 25. There were to be no festive decorations, no dancing, and no feasting or drinking of wassail, as was customary in England. In Plymouth, the colony's longtime governor, William Bradford, took a firm stand against Christmas festivities from the start. In his history of Plymouth, he describes what happened when a group of visiting non-Puritan seamen tried to celebrate Christmas shortly after the colony's founding. "The day called Christmas Day ye Governor called them out to worke," wrote Bradford, "but ye moste of this new company excused themselves, and saide it went against their consciences to work on [that] day." Bradford replied "that if they made it a matter of conscience, he would spare them till they were better informed." Then, "he led away ye rest and left them." But when Bradford and his group returned from their work, they discovered that the seamen were not observing the day with prayer and quiet contemplation, but instead were "in ye street at play openly, some pitching ye bar, and some at stoolball and suchlike sports." The outraged governor marched up to the men, "took away their implements and told them it was against his conscience that they should play and others work." As long as Bradford governed the colony, the Puritan leader observed in his history, Christmas was never celebrated again in Plymouth, "at least openly."[23]

The Minister

Governor Bradford's sternness in the matter of the seamen's Christmas was typical of the Puritan approach to life. Unsurprisingly, Puritan clergymen, or ministers, were expected to set an example for all by adhering to certain strict standards.

Puritan ministers were supposed to live in a morally upright fashion and feel personally called by God to serve the church. Just as important, they were expected to possess a thorough knowledge of the Scriptures. The minister was responsible for explaining the Bible to his flock, and for showing them how it provided guidance for every situation they might encounter in life.

To interpret the Bible as accurately as possible, a Puritan minister was schooled in Latin, Greek, and Hebrew. This knowledge allowed him to study the Scriptures and other religious texts in their original languages. Harvard, America's first college, was founded largely to ensure that the Puritan clergy received the kind of rigorous training in these ancient languages which New Englanders demanded of their ministers.

Puritan ministers dressed for church services in their regular apparel. Some wore a plain, black robe over their clothes. The Puritans did not believe in elaborate or colorful vestments for their ministers any more than they believed in decorating their churches with stained-glass windows or paintings.

Paying the Minister

In every New England town except Boston, the minister's salary was paid by public taxes.

Since hard currency was difficult to come by in seventeenth-century America, ministers often were paid with goods like beef, fish, or butter. In addition to providing them with a house, towns generally gave their pastors farmland. Consequently, many ministers received part of their compensation in donated work, such as a day's plowing or planting.

Sometimes, a minister had trouble collecting his entire salary. Indeed, this problem occurred so frequently in Plymouth that colonial officials felt compelled to issue the following decree:

> Whereas there hath been many Complaints of want of due maintainance of the ministers as some have reported; It is therefore Enacted That noe Pastor of any Congregation shall remove before his Complaint hath been Tendered to the Majestrates . . . That upon such Complaints if there appeers to bee a reall defect in the hearers of the ministers soe complaining; the Majestrates shall use all gentle meanes to [persuade] them to doe their duty heerin; But if any of them shall not heerby bee reclaimed but shall persist through plaine Obstinacye . . . then It shalbee in the power of the Majestrate to use such other meanes as may put them upon their duty.[24]

In some Plymouth towns, these "other meanes" included fining any head of household who failed to pay his ministry taxes on time double the amount owed.

The "Tithingman"

For many New Englanders, listening to their minister preach was a highlight of the week. In a world without public libraries, let alone television, radio, or the Internet, the weekly sermon served not only as a vital source of information about the Puritan creed, but also as a form of much-needed entertainment. Nonetheless, some churchgoers were evidently a great deal more interested than others in what their pastor had to say.

Since the Puritans' Sunday services lasted for up to five hours, including a two-hour sermon, it is hardly surprising that a few worshipers became fidgety, or even fell asleep, before the minister inverted the hourglass on his pulpit for the last time. Sometimes, pastors felt compelled to scold their restless flocks. The Reverend Samuel Parris of Salem reprimanded his congregation for indulging "in unnecessary gazings to and fro, or useless whisperings, much less noddings and nappings."[25]

To help handle the problem of inattentive worshipers, many New England towns appointed a special official called a tithingman. The tithingman was equipped with a long stick. A rabbit's foot, foxtail, or cluster of feathers was fastened to one end. On the stick's other end was a hard knob.

During the service, the tithingman patrolled the aisles, watching for any signs of drowsiness or restlessness among the worshipers. If a young boy or girl wriggled or whispered to a neighbor, the tithingman tapped him or her with the soft end of his wand as a gentle warning. If a woman nodded off, he roused her by tickling her nose with the same end of his stick. But if an older boy or man fell asleep or caused any sort of disturbance during the service, the tithingman rapped him sharply on the head with the hard end of his stick.

Religious Intolerance in Puritan New England

In Puritan New England, a far more serious offense than falling asleep during the pastor's sermon was daring to question the Puritan creed he taught. Openmindedness regarding different religious teachings or practices was not a virtue, as far as the Puritan leadership was concerned. Far from it. As one Puritan commentator declared: "He that is willing to tolerate any Religion . . . besides his own . . . either doubts of his own, or is not sincere in it."[26] The Puritans were convinced that theirs was the one "true" faith. They had crossed three thousand miles of ocean and risked much to build a society based on that faith. Unless every New Englander worshiped God in accordance with the Puritan creed, the Puritans assumed, their holy mission in America would surely fail. Consequently, to the creators of the "city upon a hill," religious dissenters were not just wrong. They were dangerous.

Any New Englander who challenged Puritan teachings or criticized the Puritan ministry faced expulsion. New England's two most famous religious outcasts were Roger Williams, a Puritan minister, and Anne Hutchinson, a housewife.

Williams, who questioned the close relationship between church and state in the colony and called for an end to religious intolerance, was banished from Massachusetts in 1635. But no sooner had Williams left than Massachusetts leaders found themselves confronting another rebel: Anne Hutchinson of Boston. Hutchinson boldly criticized the religious teachings of the Puritan ministry at informal meetings held in her home. Puritans often gathered in private homes to discuss spiritual issues, but dissent was not supposed to be on the agenda. When Governor Winthrop discovered what Hutchinson had been up to, he angrily banished her from the colony "as a woman not fit for our society."[27]

Another less well-known woman who incurred her leaders' wrath for questioning Puritan practices was Mary Oliver of Salem. Oliver was arrested for disrupting worship

Anne Hutchinson and the Place of Women in the Puritan Church

Anne Hutchinson's unorthodox religious views were not the only thing about her that angered Massachusetts's Puritan leaders. Governor Winthrop and the other Puritan men who ordered her expulsion from Massachusetts were also disturbed by her role as a religious teacher.

Winthrop and the others thought it was acceptable for a woman to provide spiritual guidance to other women. But the men of Hutchinson's congregation were as interested in the religious ideas she expressed at her meetings as were the women, and many attended her get-togethers. The Puritan leadership strongly disapproved of women instructing men in the Christian faith. According to the Puritan view, women were to be the followers, not the leaders, in all religious matters.

Hutchinson's independent spirit dismayed Governor Winthrop. He could find no other explanation for her behavior than mental illness brought on by excessive study. Hutchinson "hath lost her wits by giving to reading and writing," Winthrop wrote in his diary, and "she, contrary to Scriptures, rules the Roost." Winthrop is quoted in Emery Battis, *Saints and Sectaries: Anne Hutchinson and the Antinomian Controversy in the Massachusetts Bay Colony.*

Anne Hutchinson was banished from Massachusetts for criticizing the Puritan ministry.

services by declaring during meetings that everyone in the congregation, not just full church members, ought to be able to take Communion. Not long after being released on her husband's bond, Oliver was under arrest again, this time for trying to convert newcomers to the colony to her religious views. After several more run-ins with the law, the outspoken Oliver left Massachusetts for good.

Williams, Hutchinson, and Oliver got off lightly compared with the treatment of members of the Religious Society of Friends, or Quakers, as they were popularly known. Although banned from Massachusetts for preaching that churches and doctrine were obstacles to true faith, the Quakers returned to the colony time and time again. In frustration, Massachusetts leaders executed three Quaker missionaries. The hangings, which were held on Boston Commons, attracted huge crowds. As harsh as the Puritans' treatment of the Quakers

Some Quakers were executed by Puritans for preaching that churches and religious doctrine were obstacles to true faith.

may seem, many more religious dissenters were executed in the Old World than in colonial New England. Religious intolerance was the norm throughout the Western world during the Puritan era.

The Invisible World: The Battle Between Good and Evil

Evil was very real to the early New Englander, whether it manifested itself in the form of religious dissenters trying to lure believers away from the true faith, or in some quite different form. The forces of good and evil were engaged in a constant struggle for dominion over the earth, the Puritans thought. Although they believed that God and goodness would ultimately triumph, Puritans worried that Satan and wickedness might gain the upper hand temporarily.

Like most of their contemporaries, the Puritans believed in the existence of a spirit world. On the side of righteousness were the angels, God's messengers and helpers. On the side of evil were the demons. Their mission was to win converts for their master, Satan. They whispered temptation into the ears of believers wherever they might be—at home, in the field, even at church. If they chose, demons could take on the shape of a person or animal. Many Puritans reported seeing demons in the form of cats or dogs. One boy swore that one appeared to him "in the shape of a fox" and "threw him into a hogsty amongst swine."[28]

Punishments and Portents

The Puritans were quick to propose supernatural explanations for earthly events. Misfortune such as illness, severe weather, or even something as mundane as the bread failing to rise, was blamed on the devil. Since they believed they had been singled out by God to create the ideal Christian community, the Puritans reasoned that they were also bound to be Satan's favorite targets.

Perhaps surprisingly, however, the Puritans identified God as the author of unfortunate events. Just as Puritans whipped their errant children to teach them right from wrong, they saw God as a strict father who used floods, earthquakes, and other natural catastrophes to chastise his people when they sinned. Thus a persistent crop disease that drastically reduced New England's grain harvests several years in a row was interpreted as evidence of divine displeasure. Government officials proclaimed that the blight was rooted in "our manifold sins, whereby we have caused the Lord to go out against us in these yearly judgements of blasting the increase of the field."[29]

But signs from God were not always held to be punitive. In some cases, the Puritans believed, God merely wanted to warn his people to change their behavior. Then, he relied on dramatic celestial events to at-tract their attention. Comets, meteors, eclipses, and rainbows were viewed as messages from God. Ministers preached about these heavenly portents in their sermons, and diarists carefully recorded their occurrences in their journals, often in dramatic terms. "Terrible and awful"[30] is how one diarist described a comet he sighted in the night sky, while Judge Samuel Sewall characterized an eclipse as "dismal, dark, and portentous"[31] in his diary.

Witchcraft

Witchcraft, the Puritans thought, played a vital role in the ongoing battle between God and Satan. Just about everyone in seventeenth-century New England believed in witches. For centuries, witchcraft had been an important part of English folklore. Traditionally, witches were people who had signed the "Devil's Book" and pledged to be Satan's agents; Satan ensnared these weak-willed individuals by tempting them with bribes or threatening them with injury. The Puritans believed that witches targeted certain individuals and then, supposedly calling on diabolical powers, harassed these victims and their families in any number of ways. A witch might sicken a person's farm animals, cause a child to suffer an accident, or ruin crops.

Witches also were credited with the ability to "possess" their victims, causing them to suffer convulsive fits and hallucinations. Some victims temporarily lost their speech, hearing, or sight. Others suffered from a variety of bizarre symptoms. Mary Knowlton of Ipswich, Massachusetts, complained of being "pricked of her side with pins." A woman in Newbury, Massachusetts, "foamed at the mouth," according to her frightened daughter. "I was struck as with a clap of fire on the back,"[32] reported Susannah Trimmings of Portsmouth, New Hampshire, shortly after being visited in her home by a suspected witch.

Accusations of witchcraft surfaced regularly in New England throughout the seventeenth century. Over the course of the century, the number of court cases involving

The Salem Witchcraft Trials

One of the most famous episodes in New England history was the Salem witchcraft trials. The Salem witchcraft hysteria began in early 1692 when a group of adolescent girls began to suffer from convulsive fits and hallucinations. The girls were examined by a doctor and a minister, both of whom concluded that they were the victims of witchcraft. Pressured to name their tormentors, the girls accused three women. One of them, a West Indian slave named Tituba, eventually confessed to practicing witchcraft.

Accusations of witchcraft multiplied as paranoia gripped eastern Massachusetts. Between May and September 1692 hundreds of residents of Salem and nearby towns were arrested, most of them middle-aged or elderly women. A few men were also charged with witchcraft, including a former minister.

The trials themselves were highly unfair by today's standards. For example, prosecutors were allowed to introduce so-called spectral evidence, which could not be seen by any but those who claimed to be the witch's victims.

Nineteen people were hanged as witches and Giles Corey, an elderly man, was crushed to death with heavy stones for refusing to plead either guilty or not guilty. Massachusetts Bay's new governor, a non-Puritan sent to the colony by British rulers William and Mary, finally halted the proceedings. In later years, the people of Massachusetts came to regret their part in the trials. Looking back on the Salem witch hysteria, one colonist remembered the period as a time when the people walked in the clouds and could not see their way.

Witchcraft hysteria plagued eastern Massachusetts in 1692.

Of the over two hundred people tried as witches in New England during the seventeenth century, thirty-seven were executed.

witchcraft came to more than two hundred. During the same period, thirty-six New Englanders were hanged as witches, and one was pressed to death with heavy stones. A few more men and women, although convicted of witchcraft, were able to escape execution. Ironically, of those who survived, most saved themselves by confessing to be witches. Puritan judges pardoned confessed witches because they reasoned that a repentant witch could be reformed. An accused person who refused to confess to being a witch, however, posed a continuing danger to the community and, under the law, would have to die.

White Magic

Seventeenth-century New Englanders believed in the existence of good or "white" magic as well as in the bad or "black" magic practiced by witches. Puritan ministers strongly discouraged their flocks from practicing any kind of magic, white or black. Nonetheless, countless New Englanders dabbled in white magic, using charms, incantations, and fortune-telling techniques that had been practiced in England for hundreds of years.

Many New Englanders turned to charms to prevent or cure illness. Charms were prayers or spells written on papers sealed with hot wax. Reverend Increase Mather reported seeing a "sealed paper" that was sold "as an effectual remedy against the toothache, wherein were drawn several confused characters, and these words written, *In Nomine Patris, Filii, et Spiritus Sancti* [in the name of the Father, Son, and Holy Spirit], Preserve thy Servant."[33] Incantations (rhymed spells) were also chanted over a person to cure him or her of ailments ranging from fevers to warts.

Fortune-telling was also popular in Puritan New England. Some people relied on palm reading to foretell the future. Others used everyday household objects to try to answer questions regarding future events or to locate a lost person or belonging. One technique was to insert a key at random into the pages of a Bible, then ask a question. When the Bible was opened to the page marked by the key, the answer could be found in the verse to which the key pointed. Another technique called for two people to balance a sieve between the blades of an open pair of scissors, pose the problem, and interpret the wobbly move-

ments of the sieve as the answer. Rebecca Johnson told a Salem court about using the sieve method to discover if her missing son "was alive or dead." As she and her daughter balanced the sieve between them, she chanted the words, "By Saint Peter and Paul, if [the child] be dead let this sieve turn round." And "so the sieve did turn,"[34] Johnson testified, leading her to the conclusion that her son had perished.

Puritans attempted to use white magic to protect themselves and their families from suspected witches as well. Surrounding the house with cuttings from certain types of plants was said to keep witches from entering the home. Nailing a horseshoe over the front door was also believed to scare off witches. One woman who suspected that her mother had been bewitched by a certain Goodwife Morse was prompted by a neighbor to nail a horseshoe over the threshold. Later Morse was tried for witchcraft and the superstitious daughter testified that "while the horseshoe was on," Morse "would never be persuaded to come into the house . . . but she would kneel down by the door and talk and discourse, but not go in—though she would come oftentimes in a day."[35]

New Englanders also relied on "good" magic to detect witches in their communities. Something belonging to a suspected witch's victim—a lock of hair or a cap, for instance—would be burned. If the victim was an animal, a piece of its tail or ear might be cut off and thrown into the fire. Supposedly, when this magical ritual was performed, the witch would feel and behave as though she herself was on fire.

Although New England's Puritan ministers accepted the existence of witchcraft— the Reverend Cotton Mather even wrote an entire book about it—they opposed any use of magic to detect or combat witches. The evil power of witchcraft could only be overcome by prayer and fasting, the ministers insisted. Magic, they warned, was a dangerous invitation to Satan, and could never be truly "good," even when practiced by people whose motives were above reproach. As the Reverend Increase Mather, Cotton Mather's father, explained regarding the perils of magic, many innocent people "practise such things in their simplicity [naïveté], not knowing that therein they gratify the Devil."[36]

Working

Work was vitally important to the Puritans. Most settlers labored nearly every waking hour to ensure their own and their family's survival. For the Puritans, religion and the work that filled their days were intertwined. All of a believer's life belonged to God, they maintained, including his or her labor.

According to the Puritans, every person was "called" by God to work at a particular vocation. God called some to be farmers, others to be carpenters or blacksmiths, still others to be teachers or ministers. Most women were called to work within the home, feeding, clothing, and caring for their families. All work, no matter how humble, had dignity and value as long as the laborer strove to serve God in whatever he or she did, the Puritans believed. In God's eyes, all callings were equal, said the Puritan writer William Perkins, "though it be but to sweep the house or keep sheep." [37]

Start-Up Farmers: First Tasks, Essential Tools

The great majority of seventeenth-century New Englanders were yeoman farmers, meaning that they earned their living by farming their own land. Back in England, few citizens possessed land. Most farmers cultivated land they rented from a landlord. In sparsely populated New England, however, land ownership was within the grasp of nearly every adult male.

Clearing his fields was the Puritan farmer's first task after he took possession of the plot of land assigned to him by his town. Most likely, the bulk of his acreage would be heavily forested. That meant that he would have more than enough wood for building his house and barn as well as for cooking and heating. But the new farmer soon discovered that clearing forested land was slow, backbreaking work. Scores of trees had to be felled and hauled away.

Puritan farmers often "girdled" the largest trees on their plots, rather than chopping them down. To girdle a tree, a farmer cut a deep incision around the base of the tree. In time, the tree lost all its vegetation and died. Minus its leaves, the tree could be left in place without blocking sunlight needed by the crops. Farmers determined to follow the English custom of plowing their fields in straight lines, however, uprooted the tree stumps. Uprooting stumps was a difficult job, however, even for those colonists who owned teams of oxen. Consequently, many farmers simply plowed around them.

Another obstacle new farmers faced were the large stones and rocks that peppered New England's soil. They had to be pried out of the ground and rolled away before the farmer could plow his fields. Often, the farmer made practical use of the rocks by building stone walls which served as boundary markers.

Farm tools in seventeenth-century New England were few and frustratingly inefficient. Two essential tools of the Puritan farmer were the plow and the harrow. Plows were usually made of wood with an iron plowshare for cutting up and turning the hard New England soil. A farmer was doing well if he could plow just one acre of his land a day with a simple plow of this type.

After plowing his fields, the farmer went over them with a harrow, a heavy tool with spikelike teeth for pulverizing clods of earth. Most of the harrows owned by Puritan farmers were crudely fashioned from brushwood. Due to the high cost of iron in the colonies, the harrows had wooden rather than more durable iron teeth.

Most early New Englanders owned a variety of other simple agricultural tools including hoes, rakes, shovels, pitchforks, and scythes, which had long, curved blades for cutting hay and wheat. The majority of these tools were constructed entirely from wood.

Living Off the Land

The Puritan farmer faced numerous challenges. Rocky soil and inefficient tools made his job difficult and tedious. A host of predators feasted on his crops, including rabbits, raccoons, crows, and pigeons. Long New England winters made for significantly shorter growing seasons than he had enjoyed back in England.

A woman demonstrates the planting methods of the Puritans at a reconstruction of Plymouth Plantation.

Soil exhaustion was another problem that plagued the Puritan farmer. Unaware of the importance of crop rotation, farmers depleted their soil by planting the same crop in the same spot year after year. One disillusioned settler complained that the soil "after five or six years . . . grows barren beyond belief; and . . . puts on the face of winter in the time of summer."[38] English Puritans considering emigration were warned not to expect to make their fortune in New England, at least not if they planned to farm. In a pamphlet entitled *The Planters Plea*, John White of Dorcester, Massachusetts, candidly informed his fellow Puritans in the old country: "There is nothing to bee expected in New-England but competency to live on at the best, and that must bee purchased with hard labour."[39]

Following the example of the Native Americans, Puritan farmers devoted much of their farmland to corn, a crop that produced large yields, even as it made heavy demands on the soil. Although corn remained the most popular crop in New England throughout the seventeenth century, Puritan settlers also grew peas, beans, squash, wheat, and rye. Most also raised livestock.

The early settlers of Massachusetts brought hundreds of animals across the sea with them to their new homeland. As livestock were both abundantly useful and relatively easy to feed, care for, and supervise, they could be found on nearly every New England farm. Puritan farmers raised cattle for milk and beef, sheep for mutton and wool, chickens for eggs and meat, oxen and horses for pulling carts and plows. Pigs were widely owned because they could fend almost entirely for themselves by foraging in the woods for food.

To Market, to Market

During the first years of settlement, few New England farmers produced more food than their families could eat. As William Hubbard, author of an early history of New England, explains, in the beginning "the straits of the whole country were such, that every Plantation and family had enough to do, to know how to subsist."[40] As additional acreage was cleared, however, more and more farmers found themselves with modest surpluses of grain, vegetables, and livestock.

Even small surpluses could be traded at the local store for items families needed but could not make at home. These included nails, guns and ammunition, iron pots and pans, needles, and salt for preserving meat. Occasionally, farmers bartered part of their surplus for luxury items such as sugar. Cattle and beef were common and particularly lucrative commodities for New England's farmers. As the Puritan writer Edward Johnson notes in his account of New England, it was "the common practice of those that had any store of Cattle, to sell every year a Cow or two, which cloath'd their backs, fill'd their bellies with more varieties than the Country of itself afforded, and put gold and silver in their purses besides."[41]

Puritan farmers often were able to make a greater profit from their surplus timber than from their crops or livestock. Most had more timber on their land than they could use themselves. During the off-seasons, they spent countless hours cutting and hauling lumber. Some farmers fashioned the timber into shingles or other wood products, which were eagerly snatched up by merchants in Boston and other port towns for domestic and foreign markets.

Farmers who lived in coastal areas had another way to earn extra income during the off-season. They fished. The cod and other fish they caught were dried, preserved in salt, packed into wooden barrels, and sold to inland or overseas buyers. Dried fish was a pop-

Boston was the busiest port town in New England in the seventeenth century.

ular product in the seventeenth century because it provided a relatively cheap source of protein.

The Port-Town Merchant

To market their farm produce, timber, and fish, Puritan farmers relied heavily on a small but important group of fellow New Englanders: the port-town merchants who worked primarily out of Salem, Newport, and Boston. Throughout the 1600s, the busiest of New England's port towns was Boston. Stimulated by its expanding trade, Boston became the region's one true metropolis, with a population of about three thousand by midcentury.

The port-town merchant's headquarters was at the water's edge. There he supervised the loading and unloading of his fleet of sailing ships at the town wharf or at his own private wharf. Near the wharf was the merchant's warehouse, where he stored all sorts of goods from fish to wheat, before sending them off to domestic or foreign markets. Also located nearby was the merchant's countinghouse, where the merchant haggled with farmers and customers over prices or credit and hired his ships' crews.

A port-town merchant's life was filled with anxiety. Communication with overseas business partners was slow and uncertain. Keeping track of ships at sea was all but impossible. Once a merchant's ships were out of sight, many months might pass before he knew whether they had reached port safely. Countless merchant ships never did make it to their destination. Some were sunk by pirates, others were lost in storms at sea.

Lifestyles of the Rich and Mercantile

Despite the challenges they faced, many port-town merchants managed to build successful businesses. And prosperous Puritan merchants in Boston and other port towns relished showing off their newfound wealth. Boston's mercantile elite lived in "splendid and showy" mansions of brick and stone, according to one British observer, while another English visitor to the city noted admiringly that the merchants' "houses are handsomely furnished as most in London."[42] The city's wealthiest merchants also owned elegant coaches. Charles Hobby, for instance, rode about Boston in a "Coach drawn with six Horses richly Harnessed,"[43] according to a contemporary.

As the port-town merchants prospered, they earned the resentment of many of the country folk who supplied them with timber and other goods. The merchants' small-town critics complained about their luxurious houses and penchant for the latest English fashions. To some, the high-living Puritan merchants seemed to have lost sight of the real reason for the founding of the "city upon a hill." "New England was originally a plantation of Religion, not a Plantation of trade. Let Merchants . . . remember this,"[44] the Reverend John Higginson thundered in a sermon that was later published. When the rich merchant Robert Keayne was convicted of overpricing nails, buttons, and thread by a matter of pennies, he was fined the huge sum of two hundred pounds and publicly censured by his Boston congregation. Even so, many people thought Keayne got off too lightly. They said he should have been whipped as well.

Yet if ordinary Puritans decried the materialism and greed of the merchants, they were not about to stop doing business with them. Nearly everyone in seventeenth-century New England depended on the port-town merchants for vital goods that they did not have the time or resources to produce themselves.

The Housewife's Work

The work of most female New Englanders revolved around their homes and families. The majority of Puritan women married in their early twenties and had between seven and ten children, giving birth about every two years. Caring for babies and young children took up much of a woman's time and energy. The rest of her waking hours were filled with an endless round of household chores.

Housework was hard physical labor in seventeenth-century New England. Cooking was done at a blazing fireplace and included much stooping and lifting of heavy iron pans and kettles. Washing the family's clothes involved backbreaking labor, too. Pail after pail of water had to be hauled to the fireplace from a well or nearby stream. After the water was heated to near-boiling, it was poured into great wooden tubs. Up to their elbows in scalding water, Puritan housewives pounded and scrubbed their family's clothes, using soap they had made themselves from animal fat. Getting clothes clean usually took multiple washings and rinsings.

Cleaning house was also exhausting work. Sweeping was a constant chore because wood chips, pine needles, and insects inevitably fell off the incoming firewood and onto the floor. During the winter, when the house was kept tightly closed up, soot and smoke from crackling fires ended up on every exposed surface in the house, including the walls and the people's clothes. Warm weather brought its own problems. When the house was opened up in the spring, flies and other insects entered through the unscreened windows and clouds of dust from nearby dirt roads blew in on every breeze.

"A Woman's Work Is Never Done"

The Puritan housewife, always busy, filled her days with a myriad of chores in addition to cleaning and cooking. One of the most vital of these was keeping the fire in the hearth from going out. Matches had not yet been invented and striking a fire with a flint and steel could be a frustrating task. To keep fires going,

Washing a Puritan family's clothes required scrubbing and pounding the clothes using a washboard and a tub.

women fed them with wood all day long. But since blazing fires left unattended were dangerous, each night before going to bed housewives raked up the hot coals, then covered them with a thick blanket of ash, hoping that a few buried ashes would still be red-hot the next morning. If the fire went out overnight, the housewife or one of the children would trudge to a neighbor's house with a metal "fire pan" and ask to borrow some hot coals.

Among the Puritan housewife's other tasks were making candles, churning butter, milking the cows, hauling water, and tending the orchard and the kitchen garden. She was also responsible for the poultry: Not only did she feed the chickens and make sure that their eggs were gathered daily, but she also caught, killed, cleaned, and plucked them for the family table.

Puritan women devoted countless hours to their family's wardrobes, whether cutting out and sewing new garments, mending ripped clothing, or altering too-tight gowns or breeches for growing children. Many evenings were spent knitting or quilting by the fire. Two tedious and extremely time-consuming chores that most Puritan women were spared, however, were spinning thread and weaving cloth. Using the inventories of household belongings that were always taken in colonial New England following a homeowner's death, historians have been able to determine that few New Englanders owned either a spinning wheel or a loom until the final years of the 1600s. Rather than produce their own cloth at home, the majority of Puritan colonists chose to trade their surplus crops and livestock for imported cloth. As the Puritan historian Edward Johnson notes, most early settlers found it more expedient to "put away their cattel and corn for cloathing, then to set upon making of cloth."[45]

The Rhythms of Men's and Women's Work

Puritan men and women worked according to very different rhythms. A woman's chores were generally the same from one day to another. Always there were meals to prepare, fires to be banked, floors to be swept, children to be cared for, cows to be milked. A man's jobs, however, changed with the sea-

Making Bread

One of a Puritan housewife's most important tasks was making bread for her family. Bread was a staple of the early New Englanders' diet, and their techniques varied little from modern home-baking methods. Women started the breadmaking process by mixing the "sponge," a dough made from flour, warm water, and yeast (to make the bread rise). Her yeast might have come from a bit of dough saved from the last time she made bread, or perhaps from the foam floating on the top of fermenting beer.

The sponge was allowed to rise overnight in a warm, draft-free spot near the fireplace. Then the dough was kneaded, shaped into loaves, and left to rise again. Finally, it was placed into a carefully heated bake oven built into the rear of the fireplace. A flat wooden shovel called a bread peel was used to slide the loaves in and out of the oven.

Historians have determined that few Puritan women spun thread or wove cloth, and instead traded surplus crops and livestock for imported cloth.

sons. During the spring, men's days were filled with plowing and planting. During the summer they tended their fields, pruning, weeding, and scaring off predators.

Fall, which brought the annual harvest, was usually the most hectic time of the year for the farmer. Sometimes, there was too much work for the farmer to handle alone. Then his wife would have to add working in the fields to her long list of chores. During the harvest season, another common way for the farmer to manage his greatly increased

America's first female poet was Anne Dudley Bradstreet. Bradstreet immigrated to

The title page of Anne Bradstreet's collection of poetry, The Tenth Muse, Lately Sprung Up in America.

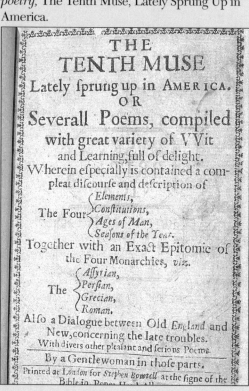

Massachusetts in 1630 as part of John Winthrop's group. Although the mother of eight, she somehow managed to find time in her hectic schedule for writing. Her first and most famous collection of poetry, *The Tenth Muse, Lately Sprung Up in America*, was published with the assistance of her brother-in-law, the Reverend John Woodbridge, in 1650. The following quotations are from *The Works of Anne Bradstreet*, edited by Jeannine Henseley.

In the preface to *The Tenth Muse*, Woodbridge took pains to explain to Bradstreet's readers that his tireless sister-in-law never skimped on her household responsibilities, despite her commitment to writing. "These Poems," he wrote, "are the fruit but of some few houres, curtailed from her sleep and other refreshments." Bradstreet herself was aware that by her insistence on writing, she was going against the grain of Puritan culture. In one of her poems, she referred to the disapproval she felt from a society that believed women should devote themselves completely to home and hearth: "I am obnoxious to each carping tongue / Who says my hand a needle better fits."

workload was to "exchange" labor with his neighbors. Nearby farmers helped one another thresh wheat or mow hay. Occasionally, neighbors also helped each other slaughter and butcher livestock. In late fall farmers traditionally killed enough of their cows and pigs to provide meat for the year ahead.

The pace of life slowed for farmers during the winter. During the cold months, men cut timber; made repairs to their houses, barns, and fences; whittled wooden bowls, spoons, and other household items; and cleaned tools.

A woman's workload remained essentially unchanged, however, with the Sabbath being the only day of the week when she could count on some respite from her usual exhausting routine.

Women Who Worked Outside Their Homes

Married women seldom worked outside their own homes in Puritan New England. Few had the time. Those who did work outside the home were usually midwives, who assisted other women in childbirth, and proprietors of dame schools, small private schools where young children were taught to read and write.

In port towns, some wives of ship captains helped to support their families while their husbands were away on voyages by operating small shops attached to their homes. For instance, in Salem, a sea captain's wife named Hannah Grafton managed a retail store next to her house while her husband was at sea. There she sold hardware like door locks and nails as well as thread, cloth, and pins imported from England.

Single women had few career opportunities in Puritan New England. Most lived with relatives, helping out with household chores in exchange for room and board. Unmarried women with no relatives to take them in usually found employment with a local family as live-in servants. Room and board was typically their only compensation.

Artisans

Few artisans (craftspeople) were able to earn a living solely off their trade in Puritan New England. Throughout much of the seventeenth century, only Boston was large enough to support full-time craftspeople. Consequently, most Puritan artisans farmed in addition to practicing their trade. Some diversified even further by taking up more than one trade. For example, the inventory of the belongings of farmer and shoemaker Joseph Coleman taken after his death reveals that Coleman owned "Cooper stuffe," indicating that he made and sold barrels as well as shoes when he was not farming.[46]

Coopers, who fashioned barrels from narrow pieces of wood called staves, were among the most essential skilled workers in Puritan New England. Their services were vital because the colonists used barrels to store and ship all sorts of goods. Other important craftsmen in early New England were carpenters, who built houses and public buildings like meetinghouses, and blacksmiths, who forged iron into items for household and farm use.

Blacksmiths repaired tools and made items such as nails, locks, and hinges.

Every New England town needed a skilled blacksmith. In his shop, he fashioned nails, locks, hinges, and other kinds of hardware, pots and pans, wheel parts, and shoes for oxen and horses from molten iron. He also made and repaired a wide variety of tools used by farmers and by other craftspeople. Usually his shop included a special wooden frame designed to confine horses while he trimmed their hooves and nailed on the iron shoes he produced.

In Boston and other seaports, dozens of different artisans served New England's booming shipbuilding industry. A host of specialized woodworkers constructed the great vessels needed for overseas trade. Craftspeople involved in outfitting the ships included ropemakers; sailmakers; tinsmiths, who made the ships' lanterns; and shipsmiths, who forged iron into anchors, chains, and other nautical hardware.

The Luxury Trades

During the first years after the founding of New England, settlers struggling just to survive had little use for the so-called luxury crafts. But by the end of the 1600s, artisans in a variety of luxury trades had opened shops in Boston and other prosperous port towns.

Wigmakers, goldsmiths, and milliners (makers of women's hats and other accessories) found loyal customers among the port towns' affluent and fashion-conscious residents. Cabinetmakers (makers of fine furniture) were in particular demand. Few Puritan settlers could afford to bring their furniture with them when they sailed to New England because of high shipping costs. Consequently, those with extra income often chose to spend it at the local cabinetmaker's

shop, purchasing chairs, tables, and other furniture of far better quality than they themselves could make at home.

Boston became particularly famous for another luxury trade, silversmithing. By the end of the century, the city supported twenty-five silversmiths, who supplied beautifully wrought silver cups, spoons, and candlesticks to well-to-do Puritans throughout New England. When wealthy Peleg Sanford of Newport, Rhode Island, wanted a silver cup made, he asked a relative in far-off Boston to make arrangements for him with a local silversmith. "Cousin," wrote Sanford, "I pray send my wine Cupp from Mr. Hull."[47]

Laborers and Servants

The majority of adult males in seventeenth-century New England were self-employed, whether as farmers, artisans, or professionals. But not every New Englander was able to work for himself. "Laborers" hired themselves out to others for daily or monthly wages. These unskilled or semiskilled workers often lived in ports like Boston, where they could easily find employment in shipyards and ship-related industries.

Even further down on New England's economic ladder were indentured servants: men or women who promised to work for an employer for a certain number of years (often seven) in exchange for passage to America. Indentured servitude was a twenty-four-hour-a-day job. Servants were not supposed to leave their master's house without permission. Thus an indenture contract drawn up between Arthur Loe of Plymouth and his master John Dingley stipulated that Loe could "not absent himselfe from . . . service by night or day, without [Dingley's] consent."[48]

Demonstrating the trade of the silversmith, a man working at Colonial Williamsburg hammers on a tumbler.

According to Massachusetts law, an indentured servant "must not be sent away empty"[49] at the end of his or her term. That is, all indentured servants were guaranteed

some form of "freedom dues" after completing their term. These were usually agreed upon when the servant was hired and could consist of anything from money

Slavery in Puritan New England

The first African slaves arrived in New England as early as 1638. Yet slavery was never a major factor in the economy of the Puritan colonies. By 1700, only about one thousand blacks lived in New England, not all of whom were slaves.

Unlike the South, New England did not have a highly lucrative "cash crop" like tobacco, which depended on big-scale cultivation by gangs of workers. A few large farms in Massachusetts and Connecticut did use small numbers of slaves as fieldworkers, but they were the exception to the rule. The relatively small number of slaves who were brought to New England were most often owned by ship captains and resided in seaports like Boston and Newport. Typically, the slaves' owners "rented" them out for specified periods of time to work in shipyards or ship-related industries such as rope- or sailmaking.

No prominent Puritan clergyman spoke out against the institution of slavery during the seventeenth century. Some clergymen, however, did urge that New England's blacks, free and unfree alike, be given greater educational opportunities.

to seeds to clothing. Freedom dues were seldom generous. For example, Margery Bateman of Charlestown, Massachusetts, was rewarded by her employer with one "she-goat" at the end of her term of service. William Snow of Plymouth did better for himself when he was freed. He received from his master "one lively cow calf of two months old, and eight bushels of Indian corne, and a sow pigg," as well as two suits of clothing.[50]

A Servant Shortage

Compared with the southern colonies, few indentured servants came to New England. Most immigrants to the region were middle-class artisans or farmers who could afford to pay their own way over. Consequently, Puritan New England suffered from a chronic shortage of servants. As one well-to-do Bostonian complained in a letter to a relative: "Our maide is gone home, and we have no body, nor can't get help for money."[51]

To cope with the servant shortage, New Englanders sometimes resorted to using forced labor. Single men or women convicted of drunkenness, petty theft, or other minor crimes might be ordered to live with a local family for a specified number of years as their servant. Webb Adey of Plymouth, for instance, was sentenced to work as a servant in the Prence household for two years after being charged with "living in idleness and nastiness."[52]

The most common source of servants in Puritan New England, however, were young orphans or children from families that had fallen on hard times. Widowed mothers sometimes "put out" one or more of their children to work in a more prosperous family's home in return for room and board. Often, very large families sent some of their offspring into servitude as well, giving themselves fewer mouths to feed. The parents of seven-year-old Zachariah Eddy declared that they were compelled to put out their young son because they had "many children, & by reason of many wants lying upon them, so as they are not able to bring them up as they desire."[53]

Contracts for young workers often included a promise by the master to teach the child to read and write. Masters were also expected to provide religious training to their child servants, and make sure they attended church services. In the Puritan view, a young servant's employer was supposed to act as a sort of surrogate parent to the boys or girls who lived and worked in his or her household.

At Home

"Well-ordered families naturally produce a good order in . . . societies,"[54] said Cotton Mather, one of the most famous Puritan ministers. Puritans were convinced that stable families were the cornerstone of stable societies. They valued the family so highly that they insisted that every settler be part of one. Barred by law from living alone, unmarried men and women were expected to live with relatives. If they had no kin in town, they were assigned to reside with local families as part of their households.

Weakness within the family was seen as a threat to the entire community. Consequently, Puritans carefully monitored what went on within every household in their towns. If problems developed within a family, town officials intervened. Parents who neglected their children's religious or moral training were warned to change their ways. If they failed to comply, officials had the right to place their children in foster families. That is what happened in 1671 in Watertown, Massachusetts, when the town's selectmen determined that Edward Sanderson's two children should live with another family for the sake of "their good education and bringing up soe they may be usefull in the commonweall."[55]

Courtship and Betrothal

In seventeenth-century England, marriages were often arranged in the manner of a business deal, with the welfare of the family as a whole—and especially its financial well-being—the chief consideration. New England Puritans, however, believed that successful marriages were based on love between prospective partners. Puritan parents did not pick their children's spouses for them. Nonetheless, they could prevent their offspring from marrying someone whom they found objectionable. Shortly after Massachusetts Bay was founded, the General Court, the colony's governing body, decreed that "none be allowed to marry that are under the covert [shelter] of parents but by their consent." Plymouth Colony enacted a similar law soon after its establishment. In 1666 the Plymouth General Court fined Arthur Howland Jr. five pounds for trying to persuade Mistress Elizabeth Prence, the daughter of Governor Thomas Prence, to marry him, "contrary to her parents likeing, and without theire consent."[56]

Puritan courtship practices included no formal dating or clear rituals. Displays of physical affection between courting couples such as kissing and holding hands were frowned upon, and young men and women were given little chance to spend time alone together.

The average age at marriage was twenty to twenty-two years for Puritan women and twenty-five to twenty-seven for Puritan men, which was late by European standards. The main reason that Puritans married late seems to be a reluctance on the part of their parents to give up their adult children's labor on the farmstead. To help couples begin their new lives together, parents provided their daughters with dowries, which usually consisted of household items such as furniture or pots and kettles. Sons were typically given land and a house. When Joseph Buckland and Deborah Allen of Rehoboth in Plymouth Colony decided to marry, for instance, Buckland's father signed a contract promising to "build the said Joseph a Convenient house for his Comfortable liveing with three score acrees of land ajoyning to it."[57]

Engaged couples participated in a formal ceremony known as a betrothal. During the betrothal, the couple promised that a marriage would take place in the future. Betrothals were usually held in the bride's home and attended by family and neighbors. After the ceremony, the couple had to "publish" their intention to marry. First, they went to the town clerk and informed him of their desire to marry. Then the clerk posted an official announcement of the couple's upcoming marriage in the meetinghouse. By law, this announcement had to be "published" three Sundays before the wedding date. That way, any townsperson who knew of a reason why the marriage should not occur could voice his or her objections.

The Wedding

Puritan weddings were simple affairs usually conducted in the bride's home. Because

Puritan couples were usually married in their own homes by town officials.

Puritans considered marriage to be a civil, not religious, ceremony, couples were wed by a town official rather than by their minister.

The ceremony was often followed by a get-together at the bride's or groom's house attended by family members, neighbors, and friends. Beer, cider—or imported wine or liquor, if the host was well-off—was served. Guests were also invited to share a special wedding cake with the bride and groom.

Samuel Sewall reports in his diary that at the wedding reception of a friend's daughter, he had "Cake and Cheese to eat there, and [to] bring away."[58]

Husband and Wife

The Puritan husband/father was the undisputed master of his household. He repre-

A Puritan husband was considered the spiritual leader of his household, while his wife often oversaw its daily activities.

Women's Rights in Puritan New England

Women in Puritan New England had few rights. They could not vote in town or colony elections. They could not sue another person, testify in court, or make most kinds of legal contracts, including wills. If a married woman earned any wages, they belonged to her spouse. If she and her husband had children together, he was their sole legal guardian.

Without a doubt, Puritan New England was a man's world. But that hardly made it

unique for its time. During the seventeenth century, virtually every society, the world over, was dominated by men. And in many places, including England, women actually possessed fewer rights than they did in New England. In New England, a widow who remarried could draw up a prenuptial contract with her future husband regarding her own and her children's rights to any property she brought to the marriage. In England, this protection was not available to widows and their children.

sented his family in all legal matters and at town meetings. Most important to the Puritans, the man of the house was the family's spiritual leader. It was his responsibility to conduct daily prayer and Bible reading sessions with all members of his household, including the family's servants.

Puritans accepted as the literal truth the biblical account of God creating Eve from Adam's rib so that he would have a helpmate. Wives were considered to be intellectually and physically inferior to their husbands and in need of their protection and guidance. In the home, as in society at large, women were expected to submit to the leadership of men. The Puritan husband was not to tyrannize his wife, however. A good husband, wrote one Puritan commentator, should "make his government of her as easy and gentle as possible, and strive to be more loved than feared."[59]

Although Puritan wives were supposed to defer to their husbands in all things, in day-to-day activities, they frequently exercised considerable authority. For example, the task of disciplining the children often fell to the wife. When her husband was away from home, a wife also had to be ready to make financial de-

cisions for her household. Nor was it unusual for Puritan women to act as surrogates for their absent husbands in business matters. When Elisabeth Gilman's husband had to leave their New Hampshire home to travel to Boston, he entrusted her with handling a large sale of timber to a local customer. "Loving wife," he wrote to Elisabeth, "so order the matter thatt Mr. Tho. Woodbridge may have Twelve thousand foot of merchantable boards Rafted by thirsday night or sooner if poseble. . . .Give Receits of whatt you Receive of him or any other man."[60]

The Family Home: From Dugouts to Salt-Box Houses

After landing in the New World, the first task confronting Puritan families was to construct some sort of shelter for themselves. During the earliest years of settlement in New England, many Puritan immigrants lived in wigwams or crude dugouts patterned after Native American dwellings. Many years later, the Reverend Michael Wigglesworth recalled vividly his first primitive home in Connecticut: "We dwelt in a

Early puritan homes included wigwams and dugouts patterned after Native American dwellings.

Cellar Partly under ground covered with Earth the first winter. . . . One great rain brake in upon us and drencht me so in my bed being asleep that I fell sick upon it."[61]

As time went on, the majority of settlers progressed to small, one-room, wooden houses. To conserve heat, ceilings were low, adding to the cramped feel of these tiny dwellings. Most of these houses featured an all-purpose room called a hall, and a loft reached by a steep stairway or ladder. Typically, the loft was used as both a storage area and a bedroom for children and any servants living in the house.

The average Puritan family consisted of two parents and seven to ten children. Since the Puritan house seldom had more than two rooms, privacy was virtually nonexistent. Even more prosperous Puritan families often were crammed into two-room houses. The extra room was used as the parents' bedroom or as a parlor where the family's valuables could be shown off. Sometimes the room served both purposes, as early New Englanders saw nothing odd about keeping a bed in the parlor. Thus the estate inventory taken after the death of farmer John Pers of Watertown, Massachusetts, listed among the contents of his parlor three beds, a looking glass, and a treble viol.

As a man's family grew, he might enlarge his home by adding on a "lean-to" at the back of the house. Typically, the central portion of the lean-to was used as a kitchen. The sloping back roof of the renovated house was significantly longer than the original structure's roof, and the building now had one and one-half to two stories in the front and one story in the rear. Its new shape reminded colonists of the wooden boxes salt was kept in.

By the late 1600s, many houses in New England were being constructed in the so-called salt-box style with a lean-to as part of the original floor plan. Salt-box houses had the advantage of being less costly to build than more traditional rectangular houses.

Seventeenth-century New Englanders usually put down wood floors in their houses, although some colonists made do with packed dirt. Rugs were not placed on floors until later in the colonial period.

The Puritans' wooden houses would seem dark and gloomy to many today. Most were left to weather to a dull brownish color, for only the wealthy could afford to buy paint. Houses were as gloomy on the inside as they were on the outside. Walls were usually covered with dark, smoke-stained boards, although some wealthy Puritans did plaster and whitewash their walls. Windows were few in

Lighting the House

The typical Puritan home was a gloomy place. Most candles were made from tallow (animal fat) and provided woefully inadequate light. Tallow candles were also a nuisance in that they required constant snuffing or trimming of the burnt portions of the wick. Last but not least, they were messy; tallow candles put off a great deal of smelly smoke and dripped hot grease almost incessantly. Little wonder, then, that most Puritan households used candles only sparingly.

Sometimes the Puritan settlers made "rushlights" to light their homes. These were fashioned from a kind of grass with a hollow stem called a rush. The rush was dipped into animal grease, then set on fire. Rushlights gave off only dim light, but they had the advantage of being both easy and cheap to produce.

Early New Englanders also used small grease or oil lamps for lighting. Often fish oil was burned in these simple, metal lamps. Since fish oil burned slowly, it lasted for a long time. Unfortunately, it also smelled terrible as it was burning.

During daylight hours, people seldom lit candles or lamps. Instead, they moved their work near open windows or doors. At night, they often toiled by the light of the fireplace or even by moonlight. By bright moonshine, a person could peel apples, wash dishes, eat, and perhaps even read, sew, or do other close work.

number and remarkably small in size. The colonists probably designed them this way to conserve as much heat as possible during the cold New England winters. Most people covered their windows with glazed paper, waxed cloth, or thin sheets of animal horn. These materials allowed little light to come through but were far less expensive than glass, which had to be imported from England.

The Fireplace: Heart of the Puritan House

Every house in seventeenth-century New England had a central fireplace constructed of stone or brick for cooking the family's meals. As much as nine feet wide, these fireplaces were cavernous by today's standards.

The central fireplace was cluttered with various types of equipment. Three-legged iron kettles, pots, and pans stood in the fire. Other pots and kettles were suspended by hooks or chains from a long "lug pole" at the mouth of the chimney. Lug poles were usually constructed of wood, presenting a built-in potential for disaster. For example, a contemporary account of an incident in the home of a Captain Denney of Massachusetts relates that as the captain's children lay by the hearth, the lug caught fire, causing a kettle of boiling liq-

Every Puritan house had a stone or brick fireplace for cooking food and providing heat.

uid to spill over the youngsters, "which scalded them in so terrible a manner, that one died presently after, and another's life is dispaired of."[62]

At the base of the hearth, large andirons supported the burning logs. Along its sides were a jumble of tools for handling the fire, including tongs, shovels, and bellows for fanning dying embers. According to her estate inventory, Mistress Huit of Windsor, Connecticut, had among other fireplace tools, "A pair Andirons, 2 Brandii [a kind of trivet set on the andirons and upon which dishes could be placed], 3 pair of tongs, and Iron Spitts."[63]

Fireplaces provided the only source of heat in the Puritans' houses. Bigger houses generally had a hearth in every downstairs room and at least one upstairs. Yet no matter how many fireplaces they contained, the settlers' houses were always cold in the winter. Although most of a fire's smoke seemed to make its way into the house, most of its heat went right up the chimney. Cotton Mather complained in his diary that on frigid winter days, ink would freeze in his inkwell, even though he was writing at a table only a few feet from his fireplace.

Settles and Chests

Seventeenth-century New England houses were sparsely furnished, according to today's standards. One piece of furniture found in many Puritan homes, however, was the "settle," a special type of bench designed to be placed directly in front of the fireplace. Settles had unusually high backs and sides to block cold drafts.

Another item owned by almost every Puritan family was a large wooden chest. Since houses of the era lacked closets, chests were indispensable for storing clothes and linens as well as a variety of other items. Chests could also be used as tables or seating, on an as-needed basis.

Wealthier Puritan families also often owned a large wooden cupboard for displaying their china, glass, or silver. In addition, they sometimes possessed a sofa or armchairs upholstered in wool, leather, or fabric embellished with needlework. Prosperous Boston merchant William Paddy kept no fewer than eleven leather chairs with embroidered seat coverings in his spacious entrance hall.

If Puritan houses typically contained little furniture, they were nonetheless usually very cluttered. The hall, the large central room, was a catch-all space in which all sorts of activity from cooking to sewing to carpentry might take place on any given day, often simultaneously. According to estate inventories, Puritan halls were crammed with a variety of bulky household equipment including big wooden barrels for storing foodstuffs and other items, buckets, and churns. Hanging items such as tools, baskets, and harnesses covered the walls. Adding to the clutter were the dried herbs that Puritan housewives often hung from the rafters of the hall's low ceiling.

Beds and Bedsteads

Despite the crowding, seventeenth-century New Englanders came from a culture in which people slept in beds, and at least one "bedstead," or wooden frame designed to support a mattress, was found in many houses. Bedsteads could be elaborate and expensive pieces of furniture featuring carved headboards and tall posts. Or they might consist of no more than a long piece of

Chests stored the clothes, linen, and other items of a Puritan household and could double as tables or seats.

cord laced over a rough frame. Puritan beds were short by modern standards. Adults had to sleep half sitting up on large pillows or bolsters. People who did not own a bedstead simply laid their mattresses directly on the floor.

The most luxurious mattresses in early New England were stuffed with goose feathers. All seven of the beds in the wealthy merchant William Paddy's home had feather mattresses, and most were also covered with expensive "pintadoes"—imported cotton quilts. Most Puritans, however, slept on crude bag mattresses filled with bits of wool, dried cornhusks, cattails, or leaves. Not surprisingly, these makeshift mattresses tended to be scratchy and lumpy.

Some New Englanders were fortunate enough to possess bed draperies. These heavy curtains were hung from the corners of special four-poster bedsteads. Curtained bedsteads provided a bit of privacy to their occupants. During the winter months, they also kept sleepers warmer by protecting them from icy drafts.

Another way to stay warm on a cold winter night was to use a "warming pan." People filled these special covered pans with hot coals from the fire, then moved them back and forth under bedsheets and blankets. "Warming pannes . . . are of necessary use and very good traffick there,"[64] wrote an English merchant regarding the immense popularity of the pans in New England.

Furniture for Children

Bedsteads were usually reserved for the adults of the household. Most Puritan children slept on mattresses laid out on the floor of the loft or hall. Very young children sometimes slept in trundle beds, compact beds that could be pulled out from under a parent's bedstead at night, then shoved beneath it in the morning. Infants generally slept in cradles. Usually attached to wooden rockers, cradles had high sides and a hood to protect the baby from drafts—a real concern in the Puritans' unevenly heated houses.

Some Puritans used warming pans filled with hot coals to heat their bedsheets and blankets.

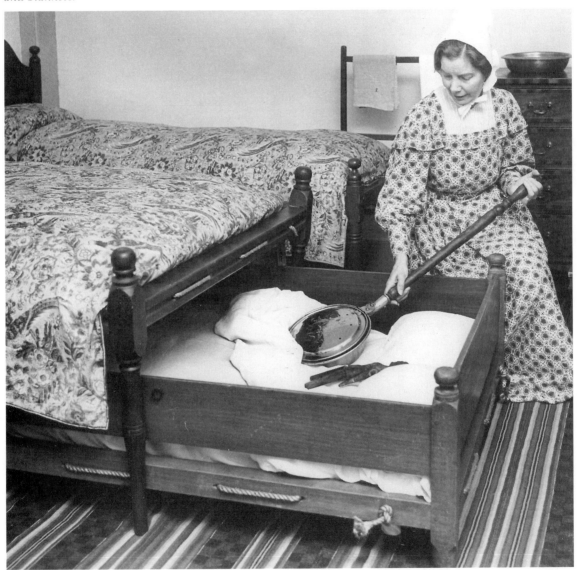

Aside from cradles, another type of children's furniture often found in Puritan homes was the "standing stool," a wooden stool with short legs and a hole cut in the seat. An older infant or young toddler was lowered into the stool's opening. The stool fit snugly around the child's waist, holding him or her in an upright position. Standing stools kept young children off of dirty floors and out of harm's way while supposedly strengthening their legs in preparation for walking.

Few Puritan families owned high chairs or child-size chairs or tables. Most Puritan fathers were too busy to make any special furniture for their children aside from a cradle or standing stool. And only a small minority of Puritan families could afford to pay a carpenter to make any furniture at all for their households, much less furniture that would eventually be outgrown.

Puritan cradles had high sides to block drafts and were usually attached to rockers.

At the Board

In most Puritan households, children and parents ate their meals at a simple plank table called a board. A board was usually constructed from one long plank, or sometimes from two planks nailed together. It rested on trestles, like a sawhorse, and could be easily dismantled for storage. For the Puritan settlers, to sit "at the board" meant to eat a meal, hence explaining the phrase "room and board"—in other words, lodging and meals. Since in most families there more people than chairs, children often sat on stools, boxes, or chests pulled up to the board. Sometimes, they even stood up to eat. If a family owned just one chair, it was customarily reserved for the father, the master of the Puritan household. From this tradition grew the phrase, "chairman of the board."

Puritan families relied on a limited range of eating utensils and dishes when they sat at the board. Spoons, the main eating utensil, were found in virtually every household. They were usually made of wood, although more prosperous families might own silver spoons. Few seventeenth-century New Englanders owned knives, and fewer yet owned forks. Such forks as could be found in Puritan New England had only two tines and were used to hold down meat while it was being cut, not to carry a piece of food to the mouth. Three-tined forks for conveying food to the mouth did not become common in any American colony until well into the eighteenth century.

Dishes came in different sizes and shapes. Most seventeenth-century New Englanders served their food on "trenchers." Trenchers were large, shallow bowls, handmade by the man of the family by hollowing out the top of a block of wood. Many families did not have enough trenchers to go around, so two or more diners often shared one.

Two employees at the reconstructed Plymouth Plantation model some of the clothing worn by Puritans.

For drinking, colonists used wooden or pewter cups. Pewter is a dull gray metal made by melting tin with copper or lead. Some people owned tankards, special mugs with hinged tops that could be flipped up for drinking. It was not unusual for a family to own just one cup or tankard. During meals, it was passed around the board from one diner to another.

The Family's Clothing

Puritans did not dress only in somber black, as many people assume today. They used vegetable dyes to color their clothing in a wide range of rich hues, including yellow, red, purple, green, and russet, a particular favorite. Black clothing was considered dressy and was worn to church services and on other formal occasions.

Clothes were made from durable natural materials such as linen, woven wool, and

Clothing and Status in Puritan New England

In seventeenth-century New England, as in most societies of the era, a person's clothing was an important indicator of his or her social rank. Puritan church and government officials believed strongly that people should dress according to their place in the social hierarchy. Dressing above one's station in life was considered presumptuous.

The Puritan governments of Massachusetts and Connecticut actually passed laws regulating which garments could be worn by the various classes of citizens. Lawmakers admonished colonists to avoid an "excess in apparel" by which people "exceeded their condition and rank" within society. In 1639 the Massachusetts General Court declared, "Our utter detestation and dislike that men or women of meane condition, educations, and callings should take upon them the garbe of the gentlemen, by the wearing of gold or silver . . . buttons . . . or to walke in great bootes, or women of the same rank to weare silk . . . hoodes or scarfes, which though allowable to persons of greater estates, or more liberall education yett wee cannot but judge it intolerable in persons of such like condition." The Massachusetts law is quoted in Stephen Foster's *Their Solitary Way: The Puritan Social Ethic in the First Century of Settlement in New England.*

leather. Cotton fabric was rarely used as it was expensive and hard to come by during the early colonial period. Because it was time-consuming to make and costly to buy, clothing was designed to last. Indeed, it was not unusual for articles of clothing to be handed down from one generation to the next in Puritan New England.

Women's Clothing

Puritan women wore gowns comprised of three parts: a long skirt, a bodice, and a set of detachable sleeves. The sleeves were tied to the bodice's armholes and topped off by shoulder pieces known as wings. Puritan women wore lots of underwear, including several layers of petticoats under their skirts and a linen chemise beneath their bodices.

On her head, a respectable Puritan woman always wore a linen cap, even in the privacy of her own home. Puritans considered bareheaded women to be highly immodest. Consequently, women carefully pinned up their long hair so that it would be completely covered by their caps.

Puritan women did not carry purses, but most did take a "pocket" with them wherever they went. Unlike pockets of today, a Puritan's pocket was a little bag, separate from the garment. The pocket was attached to a long string and tied around a woman's waist. In her pocket, a Puritan woman might store a wide variety of small, useful items ranging from keys to a ball of yarn to a baby's bib.

Women wore leather shoes, but often protected these valuable possessions from muddy roads with "clogs," a sort of half-slipper with a wooden sole. Estate inventories indicate that Puritan women commonly protected other parts of their apparel from becoming soiled by wearing aprons over their skirts and square scarves called kerchiefs around the neck, covering the upper part of the wearer's gown.

Puritan women were encouraged to dress in a plain and simple manner. Jewelry, lace, and ruffles were frowned upon. "If a woman spends more time in dressing than in praying . . . her dress is but the snare of her soul," preached Cotton Mather. Some women chafed under the Puritan restrictions on apparel. After moving to Boston, Mary Downing, the niece of Governor John Winthrop, wrote her father in London pleading with him to send her some lace with which to decorate her clothes, although "the elders with others" warned her that her lace-trimmed apparel would "give great offense."[65]

Men's Clothing

Puritan men typically wore knee-length breeches, a linen shirt, a close-fitting jacket called a doublet, a long cloak, and wool or linen stockings. Waistcoats (vests) were often worn under the doublet. Doublets, waistcoats, and cloaks were made from a wide variety of materials including canvas, wool, and, in one case at least, moose leather.

Puritan men typically wore knee-length breeches, linen shirts, doublets, and cloaks; women usually wore gowns comprised of a long skirt, a bodice, and detachable sleeves.

For formal occasions, a Puritan man might wear black shoes instead of his usual leather boots. He might also don a hat of black felt or of beaver pelts. Beaver hats were considered the height of fashion both in England and New England during much of the seventeenth century.

Children's Clothing

Puritan parents dressed all but their youngest children like miniature adults. Girls wore caps, long skirts, and layers of petticoats, just like their mothers. Boys wore breeches, cloaks, doublets, and linen shirts like their fathers. Children younger than six or seven were dressed in loose gowns, girl and boy alike. These shapeless, unisex garments had two advantages: They could be handed down from one child to another in a family regardless of gender, and they could be easily altered to accomodate a growing child.

Puritan mothers often modified the clothes of their toddlers with "leading strings" made of heavy ribbon or cord. By holding the strings, which were sewn to the shoulders of a child's gown, a parent or older sibling could gently guide the toddler's steps.

Another item of clothing designed specifically for toddlers was the "pudding." A pudding was made of thick padding that encircled a young child's head like a hat brim. It was held in place by a strap tied under the chin. The pudding protected a toddler's skull from injury while he or she was learning to walk. Puritan babies were affectionately called "puddin' head" by their parents, in reference to this protective headgear.

Growing Up Puritan

New England's Puritan leaders were deeply concerned that each new generation be prepared to carry on the work the first settlers had begun. They believed that the continued success of their "city upon a hill" depended on the moral and intellectual training which parents, teachers, and ministers provided to their community's children. During the course of their childhood, Puritan youngsters were expected to develop an unwavering devotion to their faith, respect for authority both within and outside the family, a strong work ethic, and the reading skills needed to study the Scriptures for themselves.

Disciplining Puritan Sons and Daughters

Parents bore an enormous responsibility toward their offspring, the Puritans believed. They were the first and strongest influence on their children's moral and spiritual development. If parents failed to carefully shape their children's characters, the youngsters stood little chance of ever attaining salvation. One Puritan minister painted a frightening picture of what would happen on Judgment Day to children whose parents had not trained them properly. Doomed to spend eternity in hell, the children chastised their neglectful parents, saying: "You should have taught us the things of God, and did not; you should have restrained us from sin and corrected us, and you did not."[66]

All children were born sinful, the Puritans thought. Consequently, their natural tendency was to resist their parents' efforts to teach them godly behavior. As the Puritan writer John Robinson said in a popular child-rearing manual: "Surely there is in all children . . . a stubbornness, and stoutness of mind arising from natural pride."[67]

For their own good, wayward children had to be physically punished, the Puritans maintained. For, as the Reverend Cotton Mather put it, youngsters were "better whip't, than damned."[68] Puritan parents did not rely solely on physical discipline in attempting to teach their children right from wrong, however. In hopes of ensuring their offspring's spiritual and moral development, mothers and fathers spent many hours each week with their children praying, reading the Bible, and discussing the minister's sermons.

Children at Work

Puritan parents put their children to work around the house and farm at an early age. They were convinced that hard work helped build character. Besides, running a house and a farm involved far too much work for parents to handle alone.

Children were assigned a few simple household chores by the time they were five or six years old. Young boys and girls helped their mothers weed the kitchen garden, sweep, and do laundry. By the time they turned eight, boys

Puritan children helped with household chores including weeding the garden, sweeping, and assisting around the farm.

were expected to start assisting their fathers and older brothers around the farm. Boys cared for livestock and helped to weed, plant, and harvest crops. They were also given the job of scaring off crows and other animal pests from the fields by throwing rocks at them. Cutting and hauling firewood was another task that generally fell to boys; it was an almost constant job, as families needed new supplies of firewood daily for cooking their meals and, during much of the year, for heating their houses.

By the time they were eleven or twelve, boys were considered old enough to handle a plow. At about the same age, they were also allowed to start using a gun for hunting small game or for scaring animal pests from the

fields. By the time they were teenagers, boys were expected to be able to wield a sharp sickle for cutting hay and grain and perform just about any other task around the farm.

Girls began learning the tasks of the Puritan housewife at an early age. Between the ages of six and ten they were taught to churn butter; milk cows; sew; quilt; make cheese, candles, and soap; and cook over an open hearth. Knitting was a common occupation for young girls. Girls knitted scores of stockings, caps, and mittens for their families. Many girls also spent a large part of the day supervising younger brothers or sisters.

By the age of twelve, girls were expected to be able to handle any household job. Girls from very large or poor families were sometimes sent to another household at about this age to help with child care or housework in return for room, board, and clothing.

Educating the Puritan Child

Puritans believed that every Christian needed to know how to read so that he could study the Scriptures for himself. The Puritans viewed the Bible as the ultimate authority for everything they believed and did. Only through the Scriptures could people perceive God's plan for humankind. Ministers provided vital guidance in helping believers comprehend God's holy word, but listening to a sermon was not the same as reading the Scriptures for yourself. Consequently, learning to read was considered a key part of every Puritan's upbringing.

Puritan parents were legally obliged to ensure that their children learned to read, and those who neglected these educational duties could be prosecuted. William Scant of Braintree, Massachusetts, for example, was brought before the county court on charges of "not ordering and disposing of his children as may be for their good education."[69]

Most children were taught to read at home by a parent or older brother or sister. Some Puritan children attended a dame school, however, often beginning their formal education at a very young age. Samuel Sewall's son, Joseph, for example, was not quite three years old when his father sent him off to a neighborhood dame school in Boston, "his Cousin Jane accompanying him,"[70] as Sewall noted fondly in his diary.

By the mid–seventeenth century, Massachusetts leaders had come to believe that many children were not developing adequate reading skills at their local dame school or through at-home instruction. In response, the General Court passed the "Old Deluder Law," so named because it warned that "one chief project of that old deluder, Satan" was to "keep men from the knowledge of the Scriptures."[71] To outwit Satan, all towns of fifty or more families had to set up a reading school. Any town failing to comply with the law would be fined. With the exception of Rhode Island, all the New England colonies soon followed Massachusetts's lead by mandating the establishment of reading schools in their towns.

Costs for building and maintaining reading schools were handled differently in the various New England towns. In some places, the students' parents bore most of the school's expenses through tuition fees, which were often waived for pupils from the poorest families. In the majority of towns, however, the bulk of the schools' operating expenses were paid out of public funds.

The Schoolhouse

The seventeenth-century New England schoolhouse was not designed for the comfort of the pupils. The typical schoolhouse was a cramped, single-room building with low ceilings and two or three tiny windows.

Students sat on hard, backless benches drawn up to rough plank desks. At one end of the schoolhouse was a large fireplace, the building's only source of heat. On frigid winter days, those children seated farthest from the fireplace shivered from the cold, while those seated near the fire felt half-roasted. Years later, a graduate of one of these original New England schoolhouses recalled vividly how "every cold afternoon, the old fireplace

. . . kept a roaring furnace of flame, for the benefit of blue noses, chattering jaws, and aching toes, in more distant regions of the room. The end of my seat, just opposite the chimney, was oozy with melted pitch, and sometimes almost smoked with combustion."[72]

The Schoolmaster

At the front of the schoolroom, on a raised platform, stood the schoolmaster's desk. The typical seventeenth-century New England schoolmaster was a young, unmarried man. Although women were entrusted with the running of dame schools, they were seldom hired by town officials to teach at tax-supported schools.

To most New England schoolchildren, the master was a man to be feared. Puritan teachers relied heavily on corporal punishment to keep order in their classrooms. Students were whipped with a hickory switch or birch rod for such offenses as falling asleep or giving the wrong answer. Students were also

Puritan schoolmasters punished students for falling asleep, giving the wrong answer, or behaving improperly.

expected to exhibit "good manners and dutiful behavior towards all, especially their superiors,"[73] as the town officials of Dorchester declared in their reading-school regulations. Failure to do so could result in whipping, slapping, or the application of such cruel devices as the "whispering stick," a wooden gag that was secured in the child's mouth with strings, or the "yoke," a bar with bow-shaped pieces used to hitch two young troublemakers together in the manner of an ox yoke. As a rule, parents did not object to harsh classroom discipline. In the schoolhouse, as at home, Puritans believed wholeheartedly in the value of corporal punishment for developing character in youngsters.

Hornbooks and Primers

The curriculum of elementary schools in seventeenth-century New England emphasized reading above all else. Schoolmasters gave less attention to writing and "ciphering" (simple arithmetic). Writing was considered necessary for ministers, merchants, and town officials, but not for farmers or most tradesmen. Paper and ink were expensive, and mastering the use and repair of a goose- or turkey-quill pen was difficult and time-consuming. Nor was spelling stressed in the curriculum. People throughout colonial America used "inventive" spelling. American spelling was not standardized until the late 1700s and early 1800s, when Noah Webster published his famous *Elementary Spelling Book* and dictionary.

Most students learned to read from a "hornbook," a printed alphabet sheet attached to a paddle-shaped wooden frame. The hornbook was encased in a protective covering made from animal horn that had been scraped thin until it was transparent.

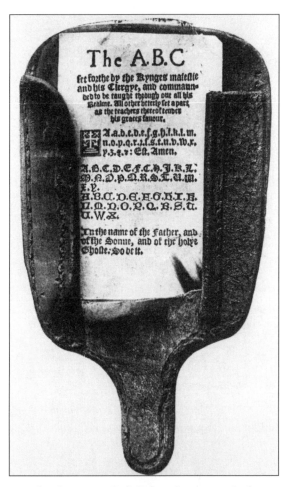

Hornbooks, printed alphabet sheets attached to paddle-shaped frames, helped Puritan students learn to read.

More advanced readers had books called primers, to help them perfect their reading and writing skills. Primers typically contained a great deal of religious material. For instance, many included the Ten Commandments and the Lord's Prayer. The most famous primer was the *New England Primer*, which first appeared in Massachusetts in the late 1600s and quickly became a best-seller. The *New England Primer* used a twenty-six-couplet rhyme to teach the alphabet, while inculcating religious and moral values. Hard work and self-discipline were encouraged

A	In *Adam's* Fall We Sinned all.
B	Thy Life to Mend This *Book* Attend.
C	The *Cat* doth play And after flay.
D	A *Dog* will bite A Thief at night.
E	An *Eagles* flight Is out of fight.
F	The Idle *Fool* Is whipt at School.

The New England Primer *contained rhymes that taught students the alphabet and religious and moral values.*

by such verses as "The Idle *Fool* / Is Whipped at school," and "*Job* feels the rod / Yet blesses God." Young children were also provided with a number of chilling reminders of the frailty of human life while they learned their letters, including the passages "As runs the *Glass* / Man's life doth pass" and "*Time* cuts down all / Both great and small." "*Xerxes* the Great did die / And so must you and I" was followed by the grim "*Youth* forward slips / Death soonest nips."[74]

Grammar School

Most children in Puritan New England did not progress beyond the rudiments of read-ing. They did not have the time. Since their labor was so often required at home, chil-dren typically spent just a few short months at school each year. Boys were needed on the farm from planting season through har-vest time, leaving them only the winter months for schooling. Girls were often needed all year long by their mothers to as-sist with the endless demands of running a household. Consequently, Puritan girls gen-erally received even less formal schooling than their brothers.

Those children who were lucky enough to continue their education beyond the elemen-tary level attended secondary, or grammar, schools. As part of the "Old Deluder Law," the Massachusetts General Court ordered all towns of at least one hundred families to es-tablish a grammar school. Other New En-gland colonies soon followed suit and established grammar schools in their larger towns as well.

Seventeenth-century grammar schools were designed primarily to be college preparatory schools. The majority of their students were male. Most often a boy started grammar school between the ages of seven and nine and studied there for seven years. The curriculum was geared to-ward the entrance requirements of Har-vard, seventeenth-century New England's only college in Cambridge, Massachusetts. Students attended classes six days a week, all year long.

Grammar schools, like elementary schools, were supported by a combination of tuition fees and tax funds. In contrast to elementary school teachers, grammar school teachers were expected to be college graduates. Many were ministers who had recently graduated from Harvard and had not yet obtained a pulpit of their own.

College Life

After completing grammar school at the age of fifteen or sixteen, a Puritan boy was ready to go to Harvard, assuming that his parents were willing and able to pay the tuition fees. Girls were not permitted to attend Harvard. No college was open to women anywhere in the American colonies or England throughout the colonial era. To progress beyond the basics of reading and writing was considered a useless luxury for young women whose whole end in life was supposed to be marriage and motherhood.

Harvard was founded in Cambridge, Massachusetts, in 1636 for the primary purpose of training Puritan ministers. Yet Harvard was never intended to be just a seminary. Many young Puritan men who had no intention of becoming ministers attended the college. The school's charter charged the institution with the promotion of "all good literature, arts, and sciences."[75] Harvard's curriculum included grammar, rhetoric, mathematics, music, astronomy, and biblical studies. All instruction was carried out in Latin.

Harvard's young scholars maintained a spartan lifestyle. Most lived in cramped and

Harvard University, founded in 1636 for the purpose of training Puritan ministers.

poorly heated dormitories. After arising early for prayers and a meager breakfast, students spent long days attending classes and studying. Evenings were taken up with more studying and mandatory prayer services. There were no organized sports at Harvard during the seventeenth century. For exercise, students took walks around Cambridge. Sometimes they spent their brief free periods fishing, one of the few recreational activities approved for pupils by the college's Puritan officials.

Unlike most colleges of today, Harvard maintained a strict dress code for its students. College students were supposed to dress in a neat and conservative manner both on campus and off. "No scholar shall go out of his chamber without coat, gown, or cloak, and everyone everywhere shall wear modest and sober habit without strange ruffianlike or newfangled fashions,"[76] declared the college laws.

Apprenticeships

Technical schools for training artisans did not exist in Puritan New England, or anywhere in colonial America or Europe during the seventeenth century. Young people were apprenticed to a local artisan in order to learn a particular trade.

If a Puritan father could spare his son's labor on the family farm or in the family business, he might "bind out" the child to a craftsman such as a carpenter, shoemaker, or cooper. The artisan would then become the child's master. He agreed to teach the boy his craft and provide him with room and board in return for labor. Often, he also had to agree to teach his apprentice how to read and write. The contract drawn up in 1690 between young William Walton of Newport and John Odlin, for instance, stated that in addition to being instructed in the blacksmith's craft, Walton would receive instruction "in ye read-

A Youthful Rebellion over Hair

In addition to its strict dress code, Harvard also had regulations regarding how students could style their hair. The school laws for 1655, quoted in James Axtell, *The School Upon a Hill: Education and Society in Colonial New England*, declared that it was unlawful for any student "to wear long hair." They were also forbidden from "curling, crisping, parting, or powdering" their hair.

Despite Harvard's rule against long hair, during the mid–seventeenth century a fad for growing their hair developed among the students. Shocked officials scolded the boys for giving up the traditional close-cropped style of their elders in order to wear their hair "like a woman's."

Eventually, the older generation of Puritans got used to the longer hairstyles favored by the college students. But no sooner had parents and authorities stopped complaining about the boys' long hair than a new fashion developed among the young people. Students began shaving their heads and wearing "periwigs," curly, shoulder-length wigs which were all the rage in England during the late seventeenth century. Older Puritan men were attracted to the new style as well, which was considered by many to be the height of elegance. Even the Reverend Cotton Mather, always outspoken in his criticism of "excessive" dressing among women, was wearing a periwig by the end of the century.

ing of English according as hee is capable for to learne."[77]

Apprentices started out by doing odd jobs and simple chores around their master's shop. Over time, they took on increasingly complex tasks, until they were eventually able to perform all aspects of the artisan's work.

Apprenticeships usually lasted for a term of seven years. Most boys began their apprenticeships around the age of fourteen so that they could be finished by their twenty-first birthday, the legal age of maturity. An apprentice owed obedience and respect to his master, who was a boy's teacher, employer, and foster parent all in one. Most apprenticeship contracts further stipulated that the apprentice could not leave his master's home without his permission, marry during the course of his term, or give away any of his master's trade secrets.

An apprentice's life was hard. Work filled his days from dawn to dusk. On the Sabbath, his one day off, an apprentice was expected to attend church with his master's family, then spend the rest of the day praying and reading the Bible. Punishments for apprentices who failed to complete their work or disobeyed their masters could be harsh. Masters were permitted to use corporal punishment on apprentices as they saw fit. And an apprentice's contract with his master was strictly binding, in sickness and in health, as the Widow Quilter of Ipswich discovered when she tried to break the contract that tied her son, Joseph, to his master, William Buckley. When Joseph fell ill, Quilter was "greeved to the harte" at the conditions she found in Buckley's house. "Fearing that he might perish," she took Joseph home. But the court had no sympathy for the widowed mother or her ailing son.[78] Despite Quilter's pleas for mercy, the boy was forced to return to Buckley to finish out his apprenticeship.

Fun, Puritan Style

Neither Puritan children nor Puritan adults had much time for recreation. Yet, there is little truth in the modern stereotype of Puritans as killjoys who did not believe in having fun themselves and did not want anyone else to have it either. Puritans did think that recreation possessed *some* value, especially for children. One Puritan author advised parents of young children that "time for lawful recreation now and then, is not altogether to be denied." Nonetheless, he went on, parents should carefully ration the amount of playtime they allowed their sons and daughters. For children "to do little or nothing else but play," he declared, "is a great sin and shame."[79]

The Puritans believed that certain forms of recreation were acceptable for people of all ages, but only if enjoyed in the strictest moderation. Obsessed with making every minute of their time on earth count, the Puritans branded idleness as evil. Thus when sixteen-year-old Elizabeth Saltonstall traveled to Boston in 1684 to visit relatives, her mother implored her to use her time away from home not for sightseeing or relaxation, but for learning how to embroider. "It would be a very great trouble to me [if] you should misuse your precious time or any way mispend it. Consider what a precious talent time is and what a strict account you must another day give for it,"[80] Mistress Saltonstall wrote to her daughter.

The Puritans disapproved of a number of recreational activities that were popular in England. They deplored dancing and stage

Puritans and Dancing

Dancing has been a popular recreational activity for young people in countless societies throughout the ages. In the seventeenth century, it was popular with all classes of young people in England, from peasants to aristocrats. But dancing was frowned upon in Puritan New England. Although no New England colony actually passed a law forbidding the activity, Puritan ministers regularly denounced dancing as immodest and as encouraging "lascivious" behavior between male and female partners.

In 1684, when a dance school for young people was opened in Boston, a prominent local minister immediately fired off a pamphlet in protest. Soon after, the school was closed. By the last years of the century, however, the Puritan clergy's crusade against dancing had been lost, at least in bigger towns like Boston. Dancing was becoming a common form of entertainment among Boston's upper classes, and the city supported several dancing schools by 1700.

plays, calling them immodest and ungodly. They forbade all games of chance (including card games) because they sometimes led to gambling. They scorned competitive sports such as tennis or bowling as frivolous and tending to encourage rowdy behavior.

Since wasting time on "frivolous" activities was a heinous sin in the Puritan view, they favored those forms of recreation which they believed to be useful. The idea of having fun for its own sake was completely foreign to them. Fishing, since it produced food, was considered a wholesome form of recreation for Puritan boys and men alike. Hunting was also acceptable for the same reason.

Reading as Recreation

Reading was one of the most productive ways in which a child could spend his or her leisure time, the Puritans believed. That is, as long as the material being read conformed to Puritan standards of morality and usefulness. Novels and most poetry were not acceptable reading material for either youngsters or adults; the Bible and religious works by Puritan authors were.

Puritan children were particularly encouraged by their elders to read a long religious poem that was New England's first best-seller. After the Bible, the most popular religious work in Puritan America was *The Day of Doom*, an epic poem of more than two hundred eight-verse stanzas. Written by the Reverend Michael Wigglesworth, the poem had a chilling theme: the physical and mental agonies suffered by sinners in hell. Puritan parents approved so heartily of Wigglesworth's spine-tingling poem that they made their children memorize lengthy passages from it, then recite its dire warnings aloud.

The effect of this terrifying reading matter on young minds can only be imagined. Perhaps Betty Sewall, daughter of Samuel Sewall, was thinking about *The Day of Doom* when she "burst out into an amazing cry," as Sewall recorded in his journal. "Her Mother ask'd the reason; she gave none;" wrote Sewall. Finally, young Betty tearfully confided to her parents that "she was afraid she should go to Hell, her Sins were not pardon'd."[81]

Another popular form of religious literature that was probably more popular with young readers was the so-called captivity narrative. These true accounts of settlers captured by Native Americans were designed to teach moral lessons as well as provide entertainment. Countless Puritan children grew up hearing the tales of warfare, imprisonment, and daring escapes which filled the typical captivity narrative.

Reading was not a solitary form of recreation for most New Englanders. In Puritan households, reading aloud was a common activity. Parents read aloud to their children; children read aloud to their parents and siblings. Long winter evenings by the fireside were a favorite time for this family-centered leisure activity.

The Productive Party

Another approved form of recreation for Puritan children and adults alike was what one historian has labeled the "productive party."[82] House-raisings and barn-raisings and "bees" were among the most common of these productive parties, at which work and play were combined.

At "raisings," townspeople came together to help a local family build a house or barn. House- and barn-raisings were festive occasions for children. The events invariably featured plenty of food and socializing. Cornhusking bees were also popular with young Puritans, especially teenagers, for they were one of the few activities in Puritan society

Stories about settlers captured by Native Americans were popular during Puritan times.

Growing Up Puritan

that permitted boy-girl socializing. The evening usually included refreshments, a bonfire, and an exciting cornhusking contest. People divided into teams and competed to see which group could shuck the most ears of corn in a set amount of time.

Berrying expeditions were another type of productive party that was particularly popular with teenagers. These day-long expeditions were usually reserved for a community's adolescent girls. Often, the berrying parties were unchaperoned, giving the girls a rare chance to socialize without adult supervision. Teenage girls also enjoyed sewing and quilting bees patterned after bees held by their mothers.

Teenage boys in Puritan New England enjoyed a different kind of productive party: the militia training-day festivities. All Puritan towns maintained a militia to protect against possible attacks by Native Americans. Every able-bodied male from the age of sixteen to sixty had to serve in his town's militia and attend training days, which were usually held at about two-month intervals. Militia members gathered at the town green in the morning and spent several hours drilling. Then the partying began. Athletic contests were held during which young militiamen could have fun while increasing their physical stamina and military skills. Foot races, wrestling matches, and target-shooting contests were favorite activities. Plenty of refreshments were always served, including beer, which was considered an acceptable drink for Puritans of all ages.

6 Health and Medicine

The Puritan settlers confronted many challenges to their health in the New World. Among them were widespread disease, poor hygiene and sanitation, unbalanced diets, dangerous childbirths, and inadequate and often harmful medical treatments. Although the average New Englander lived longer than his or her counterpart in the southern colonies, by modern standards, life spans were short and infant mortality rates high in seventeenth-century New England.

A Shortage of Doctors

In seventeenth-century England, physicians were expected to possess a medical degree from a university. In New England, only a handful of physicians held an M.D. Those few medical school graduates had earned their degrees in Europe, for there were no medical schools in the American colonies until well into the 1700s.

Physicians with diplomas from Old World universities were in high demand in the towns of Puritan New England. The officials of Newbury, Massachusetts, not only presented a large farm to Dr. John Clarke, who held an M.D. from an English university, but also promised that Clarke "in respect of his calling should be freed and exempted from all public rates either for the country or the towne so long as he shall remayne with us and exercise his calling among us."[83]

The town of Newbury was fortunate to have snagged Clarke; most Puritan communities had to settle for far less qualified physicians. Many New England physicians acquired medical skills by serving as apprentices to established practitioners for anywhere from a few months to a few years. A physician's apprentice learned by observing and assisting his master as he worked, and by studying whatever medical books he owned. Countless New England physicians could not even boast of that much training. These entirely self-taught doctors learned medicine the trial-and-error way—on their unwitting patients.

Since none of the Puritan colonies had licensing or regulatory boards for physicians, just about anyone could come into a town, call himself a doctor, and set up a practice. Nicholas Knopp, the first doctor in Boston of whom there is any record, was a charlatan. In 1630, town officials fined him five pounds "for takeing upon him to cure the scurvy by a water of no worth nor value, which he solde att a very deare rate."[84]

Confronted with a scarcity of qualified physicians in their communities, many New Englanders turned to their ministers for medical advice. Frequently the only college-educated person in his town, the Puritan minister was considered by his parishoners to be a font of wisdom on virtually every subject, including medicine. Among the many small-town Puritan preachers who took on medical duties in addition to their pastoral responsibilities was the Reverend Michael

Puritan ministers were considered knowledgeable on every subject, including medicine.

Wigglesworth, author of the best-selling poem *The Day of Doom*. When Wigglesworth died, his grateful parishoners in Malden, Massachusetts, had his gravestone inscribed with the following tribute: "Here lies intered in silent grave below / Malden's physician for soul and body two."[85]

Bleeding, Purging, and Dosing

Whether university-educated or not, seventeenth-century physicians were woefully ignorant re-garding the actual causes of disease. Most accepted the theories of the second-century Greek physician Galen. He believed that the human body was governed by four substances, or "humors": phlegm, blood, black bile, and yellow bile. According to Galen, when these humors became unbalanced, sickness was the result.

To restore balance among the humors, seventeenth-century physicians relied primarily on two potentially dangerous treatments: bleeding and purging. Convinced that excessive blood was at the root of many illnesses, physicians relieved their patients of up to two pints of blood at a time by cutting open their veins with a lancet, a small, sharp knife. Leeches, a type of blood-sucking worm, were also used by doctors to remove "excess" blood from patients. If the physician determined that the patient suffered from an excess of bile rather than blood, he would be given a powerful cathartic such as castor oil to purge the intestines. Doctors sometimes recommended that patients purge their systems of harmful bile by taking emetics to induce vomiting as well. Countless colonists died from excessive blood loss or dehydration brought on by these crude treatments.

Physicians also dosed their patients with a variety of medicines, some of which featured bizarre ingredients. One Boston doctor prescribed a syrup composed of sowbugs drowned in wine for tuberculosis (a disease that usually attacks the lungs). Dr. Winthrop, a highly respected Connecticut physician, treated his patients with medicines made from syrup of violets, powdered coral, and horseradish. Salem's longtime physician, Zerobabel Endecott, compiled a notebook of what he considered to be his most effective remedies, including the following:

For Sharpe & Dificult Travill in Women with Child [difficult labor] Take a Lock of

Second century A.D. *Greek physician Galen believed that unbalanced humors caused human sickness.*

Vergins haire on any Part of ye head, of half the Age of ye Woman in travill. Cut it very smale to fine Pouder then take 12 Ants Eggs dried in an oven . . . & make them to pouder with the haire, give this with a quarter of a pint of Red Cows milk. . .

For the Shingles [A painful viral disease of the skin] [T]ake the moss that groweth in a well & Catts blod mixed & so aply it warme to the plase whare the shingles be . . .

For the Ague (the chills) Take the Drye shell of a Turtell beat smale & boyled in water while 2 thirds of the water be consumed & drinke of it 2 or 3 times when the Ague Cometh.[86]

In most New England communities, medicines prescribed by a physician were mixed and sold by the doctor himself. In Boston, colonial New England's largest town, specialists called apothecaries sometimes compounded and dispensed medicines for local physicians. Obtaining certain medicines, particularly those that required imported ingredients, could be difficult outside of Boston. The diarist Samuel Sewall reported having to buy in Boston medicines for his mother which her doctor in Newbury, Massachusetts, had prescribed.

Surgeons and Surgery

Seventeenth-century English surgeons as opposed to physicians, did not hold university degrees. Nor were they honored with the title of "doctor." They were viewed as craftsmen—men who relied on their hands more than their brains to perform their work. In New England, where medical specialists were in short supply, the distinction between physician and surgeon was less clearcut than in the mother country. Often, a town's physician was also its surgeon.

Many other surgeons in seventeenth-century New England spent the bulk of their days working at jobs completely unrelated to the medical field. For them, surgery was a sort of sideline. All a surgeon needed to practice his craft in the Puritan colonies were the right tools—sharp knives and saws being the most essential. Surgery was performed by barbers, blacksmiths, farmers, and ship captains, among others, on an as-needed basis. Many of these part-time surgeons were self-taught; others learned their craft as apprentices to established practitioners. Typically, one of an apprentice's most important tasks was helping to hold down patients during operations. This challenging job was essential because there was no anesthesia in colonial times.

Because the relationship between microscopic organisms and infection was not recognized until the late 1800s, one task a surgeon's apprentice was never called on to do was to sterilize the surgical instruments before an operation. Consequently, many patients were infected—often fatally—by a surgeon's germ-contaminated instruments and hands.

Surgery in Puritan New England, as everywhere else in the seventeenth-century world, was primitive. Surgeons performed operations to treat wounds and broken bones, but few attempted major abdominal, chest, or head surgery. Amputations were carried out routinely to remove infected body parts. And, since surgeons did not know how to set compound bone fractures, amputation was the only remedy for badly injured limbs, as well.

During the seventeenth century, patients were often infected by their surgeons' germ-contaminated instruments.

Women and Medicine

A shortage of qualified physicians combined with high medical fees caused many New Englanders to seek medical care within their own homes. The role of household doctor was almost always assumed by the Puritan wife and mother. Women bandaged wounds, nursed the bedridden, and tended to a wide range of ailments from frostbite to indigestion. Most Puritan housewives possessed an extensive collection of "receipts" (recipes) for homemade medicines. Receipts for medicinal syrups, powders, and pastes were passed down from mother to daughter as important family traditions. Their main ingredients were usually herbs gathered from the kitchen garden or a nearby meadow or forest.

Some Puritan women practiced medicine outside of their immediate families. These self-taught folk healers provided medical care to their neighbors for a small fee. Many were respected and highly valued members of their communities. Court records testify that Anna Edmonds was so successful in treating her fellow townspeople that the citizens of Lynn, Massachusetts, honored her with the title of "doctor woman." Records also reveal that some female healers, like the Widow Hale of Boston, turned their houses into makeshift hospitals and took in sick neighbors for "nursing."[87] Hale and other Puritan women who opened their homes to sick and injured neighbors performed a vital service to their communities, since there were no formal hospitals or nursing homes in New England until well into the eighteenth century.

Midwives and Childbirth

The most common female medical practitioner in Puritan New England was the midwife. In the American colonies and in the Old World, obstetrics (the branch of medicine concerned with childbirth) was the domain of the midwife, not the physician. Most midwives had no formal medical training. Instead, they acquired their skills from hands-on experience.

Giving birth was a dangerous undertaking in Puritan New England and everywhere else in the world in those days. One in five women in New England died from causes related to childbirth during the 1600s. Little wonder, then, that many women anticipated childbirth with dread. In her poem "Before the Birth of One of Her Children," a pregnant Anne Bradstreet addressed the following verses to her husband: "How soon, my Dear, death may my steps attend. / How soon't may be thy lot to lose thy friend."[88]

To offer encouragement and comfort to the anxious mother-to-be, female relatives and neighbors usually attended births along with the midwife. Sarah Smith, the wife of a Puritan minister in Falmouth Neck, Maine, went so far as to invite all the married women living in her town to join her for the birth of her sec-

Cotton Mather and the Smallpox Innoculation Controversy

When fifteen-year-old Cotton Mather wrote his grandfather about the smallpox epidemic ravaging his hometown, he could not have dreamed that someday he would make an important contribution to the control of the deadly illness. More than fifty years after Mather wrote his letter, another devastating smallpox epidemic struck Boston. This time, Mather, now a famous minister and scholar, had a plan for addressing the emergency.

Mather's plan centered on a folk practice he first learned about from an African slave. It involved inoculating a healthy person with fluid from a smallpox blister. The patient contracted smallpox, but in a very mild form. Like someone who caught the illness naturally and survived, the inoculated person was left with a lifelong immunity to smallpox.

Mather was able to persuade just one physician in Boston to give his idea a try. With Mather's assistance, Dr. Zabiel Boylston eventually inoculated nearly three hundred Bostonians. But instead of lending Boylston and Mather their support, the city's leading physicians accused the two men of deliberately spreading smallpox through their inoculations. Panicky Bostonians flooded Mather with hate mail. He refused to back down, however, even after someone hurled a homemade bomb into his house. (The bomb failed to explode.)

When the epidemic finally ran its course, the results of Mather's controversial experiment caused an international sensation. Just 2 percent of the inoculated Bostonians died, compared with 15 percent of those who caught the smallpox virus naturally. Soon, inoculation was being widely used throughout the American colonies and Europe. By 1800, it had been replaced with a safer smallpox vaccine which left patients with one localized blister instead of a mild case of the disease.

ond child. Mothers-to-be were expected to offer refreshments to their birth attendants. The wife of the prosperous merchant and diarist Samuel Sewall treated her midwife and attendants to a veritable feast after her delivery. According to Sewall, the women were served "Boil'd Pork, Beef, Fowls, very good Roast Beef, Turkey-Pye, [and] Tarts."[89]

Epidemics

Endemic disease (illnesses which are always around) such as pneumonia, tuberculosis, and dysentery (severe diarrhea) claimed more lives in Puritan New England than epidemic illnesses. Yet it was epidemic disease that the colonists seemed to fear most. Epidemics tended to strike a community swiftly and violently, and were usually most deadly to its youngest members. Infectious diseases like measles, whooping cough, and "throat distemper" (diphtheria) were particularly dangerous for children.

In larger towns like Boston, epidemic diseases took a terrible toll. Illness spread as effortlessly as the wind through Boston's narrow, crowded streets. In a letter to his grandfather, fifteen-year-old Cotton Mather described a smallpox epidemic that ravaged the city in 1678: "Never was it such a time in Boston. Boston burying-places never filled so fast. . . . To have coffins crossing each other as they have been carried in the street;—To have, I know not how many corpses following each other close at their heels,—to have 38 dye in one week,—6,7,8, or 9 in a day."[90]

Boston's Puritan officials tried to fight the smallpox epidemics that ravaged the city every decade or so by mandating public fast days. They enacted more practical measures to slow the spread of the disease as well, such as prohibiting those who had had the virus

Cotton Mather believed his reputation would be ruined if the public learned of his wife's insanity.

from "go[ing] abroad too soone." Citizens were also barred from hanging out the clothing and bedding of sick family members in their yards or near roadways. Several spots on the city's outskirts were set aside where people could air the infected clothing, sheets, and blankets "in ye dead time of ye night."[91]

Mental Illness

The Puritans had little understanding of mental illness or its causes. Most blamed insanity on either satanic possession or a troubled conscience. The diarist John Hull wrote regarding two women in his town who were given to "raving and madness," "Men know not the human cause. Some think . . . they were left to some notorious sin, but could not confess it; others think Satan took advantage of a spirit of discontent with their own condition, as being poor."[92]

Having a mentally ill family member was a source of shame for the colonists. Cotton Mather was terrified that his parishoners in Boston would find out about his wife's periodic bouts of insanity. In his diary, he confided: "I have lived for near a year in a continual anguish of expectation, that my poor wife by exposing her madness, would bring a ruin on my ministry."[93]

New England had no institutions to house the mentally ill. People were expected to take their disturbed kin into their own homes. If a mentally ill person did not have relatives nearby, the government intervened, assigning the individual to live with a local family and compensating that family for his or her room and board.

Hygiene

Seventeenth-century New Englanders were as ignorant about the importance of personal hygiene as they were of the causes of mental illness. Like most other people of their time, the Puritans were a dirty and, no doubt, smelly lot. Disease-carrying lice and fleas lived in their hair, clothing, and bedsheets. Deodorant was unknown, and people almost never bathed. The daily cleansing ritual of most early New Englanders probably consisted of a quick hand rinsing and a splash of cold water on the face from a bucket kept by the back door.

People seldom washed their entire bodies. Indeed, bathing was considered an unhealthy practice; it supposedly depleted the skin of protective oils, opening the pores to disease-causing "vapors." There were other reasons the Puritans avoided bathing. For one thing, privacy was in short supply in crowded Puritan homes. For another, water to fill the big wooden tubs used for bathing had to be hauled in buckets from a well or nearby stream, an exhausting and time-consuming job. Then, unless the bather was unusually hardy, the water had to be heated over the fireplace before being poured into the tubs—another time-consuming task.

When people did bathe, it was often without the benefit of soap, which was saved for scrubbing dirty clothes. Soap was usually made at home from animal fat and lye, a harsh substance derived from wood ash. When used on the body, the homemade soap left a person's skin red and irritated.

Puritans used soap even more sparingly on their dishes than on their bodies. Indeed, people did not believe in wasting soap on dish washing, merely wiping down cups and other tableware with a rag. Badly soiled cooking utensils were sometimes dragged to a nearby stream, where they were rubbed with gravel or sand to remove burned-on food. And since the idea of contagious diseases had not yet been developed, Puritan diners thought nothing of sharing their cups and spoons.

Sanitation

With no running water, hence no indoor plumbing, people were forced to rely on "privies" (outhouses) and chamber pots. Outhouses were often located dangerously close to the family's water supply. Many a well or stream was tainted by human waste, explaining in large part why dysentery was a leading killer in seventeenth-century New England. To dispose of garbage, people just tossed it out their windows and doors into their yards or a nearby road, a habit that the first immigrants brought with them from England.

Poor santitation was a particularly serious problem in bigger towns such as Newport and Boston. In Newport, one town official complained, some streets were nearly unpassable, "as several Privy houses sett against ye Streets" emptied into the roads, placing pedestrians in continual danger of "Spoiling & Damnifying" their apparel. In Boston, thoroughfares were strewn with rubbish and refuse of all sorts. On more than one occasion the city government instituted laws prohibiting the disposal of garbage in the streets. The casting of animal carcasses onto the streets was specifically addressed by the selectmen. No "intralls [entrails] of beast or fowles or stinkeing thing" were to be tossed into the roads, the officials declared. Instead, they were to be dumped into a creek on the outskirts of the city. As far as other kinds of refuse was concerned, inhabitants were instructed to "bury ye same."[94]

Boston's officials also hired scavengers to rid their streets of debris. These workers were aided in their task by the city's resident animal scavengers: the hogs who roamed Boston's fly-infested thoroughfares at will. As in the villages of old England, few people in New England bothered to pen up their swine. In rural areas, the townspeople's hogs foraged in nearby woods for food. In cities like Boston, they foraged in the garbage-strewn roadways, often making passage of the narrow streets difficult for both people and horses. To make matters worse, the hogs deposited what probably amounted to tons of dung in the city streets each year. Time and time again Boston's selectmen voted that pigs should not be allowed to run free. Few citizens seemed to have complied with the rulings, however.

Diet

Colonial Americans, like their European counterparts, were as unaware of the role of proper nutrition in maintaining health as they were of the importance of good hygiene and sanitation.

Puritans lacked knowledge of proper nutrition and generally ate foods that contained too much animal fat and salt.

The Puritans' day-to-day eating habits would be considered unhealthy by today's standards. Generally speaking, their diet contained too much animal fat and salt and too few fresh fruits and vegetables.

Seventeenth-century New Englanders ate lots of meat compared with families in England, although except in frontier towns, few people hunted wild game such as deer or possum. Most New Englanders relied on livestock for meat, especially pigs because they were easy to raise. Puritan housewives cured hams, sausages, and bacon. They wasted nothing, even using the pig's feet for pig-foot pies. Pork or other meat was seldom eaten fresh, except during the annual livestock slaughtering in late autumn. Most of the year, Puritan families ate meat that had been heavily salted and packed away in wooden barrels to preserve it. Many people ate fish as well, which was lower in fat but also heavily doused with salt for preservation.

Except in the amount of meat they ate, most Puritan settlers copied the traditional English diet. Just as they had done back in England, the colonists planted primarily root vegetables like turnips, onions, and parsnips, then cooked them to a pulp, removing most of their nutritional value in the process. Vegetables were never eaten raw—that was considered unhealthy.

Although they clung to many of their Old World eating habits, the Puritans did adopt some new foods from the Native Americans. Pumpkins, in particular, became a staple of their diet, especially during the earliest years of settlement. "Let no man make a jest at Pumpkins, for with this fruit the Lord was pleased to feed his people to their good content, till Corne and Cattell were increased,"[95] declared the Puritan historian Edward Johnson.

The most important food that the Puritans borrowed from the Native Americans was corn. Corn, which was relatively easy to

Pumpkin became a staple of the Puritan diet after they adopted it from the Native Americans.

Puritans of all ages consumed cider and ale.

grow and yielded large harvests, soon became central to the settlers' diet. Eaten year round, corn could be steamed, roasted, or pounded into corn meal for use in breads, porridges, and puddings. Roger Williams reported that cornmeal "mush" (porridge) was a staple of the Puritans' diet, served either "hot or cold with milk and butter."[96]

Puritans did not expect their food to be interesting. Housewives made the same simple dishes for months on end, feeding their families on whatever was available. Breakfast and supper (the last meal of the day) usually consisted of cornmeal mush or bread and cheese. Dinner, the main meal of the day, was served at midday. It usually featured some

sort of stew that had been simmered in a big kettle for hours. The stew's ingredients varied with the season, but it generally included a meat and one or more root vegetables like turnips or parsnips.

Ale and Cider

Cider and ale were the main beverages of Puritans of all ages. Milk was seldom drunk, even by children; usually, it was made into butter or cheese. Puritans also rarely drank water, a habit they had brought with them from England, where most rivers, streams, and lakes were too polluted to drink from.

Tobacco in Puritan New England

Tobacco smoking was common in Puritan New England. During the seventeenth century, many people believed that tobacco was beneficial to the health. John Josselyn, an Englishman who traveled extensively in New England and the other American colonies, summarized the supposed health benefits of the tobacco plant in his best-selling book *An Account of Two Voyages*. "The virtues of Tobacco are these, it helps digestion, the Gout, the Tooth-Ache, prevents infections by scents," he wrote in a widely read account of his travels published in 1674. Moreover, he assured his readers, "It heats the cool and cools them that sweat, feedeth the hungry, spent spirits restoreth, purgeth the stomach, killeth nits and lice." Josselyn's book is quoted by George E. Gifford in his "Botanic Remedies in Colonial Massachusetts" in *Medicine in Colonial Massachusetts*.

Few early colonists drank beverages made with heated water, either. Tea and coffee did not become popular in America until well into the eighteenth century.

Although some Puritan towns had breweries, most people brewed their own ale at home. Drunkenness was frowned on by the Puritans, so ale was seldom consumed in excess. The colonists were convinced that a moderate amount of ale each day promoted good health. A New England almanac from 1688 included the following poem extolling the benefits of ale: "January's Observations. / The Best defence against the Cold, / Which our Fore-Fathers good did hold, / Was early a full Pot of Ale, / Neither too mild nor yet too stale."[97]

While many children drank diluted beer with their meals, cider was a more popular drink for youngsters and it was widely consumed by adults, as well. Cider was generally made from apples, although pears were also used. Cider was an alcoholic drink in Puritan New England, although it usually had a lower alcohol content than ale or beer. The cider's alcohol content was the result of the natural fermentation of the apple or pear juice.

Death in Puritan New England

The pall of death was ever present in Puritan New England. Disease, childbirth, and accidents claimed numerous victims—young and old—every year in every town.

Since the Puritans believed that elaborate funeral services were "popish," their burial customs were simple. When a person died, he or she was wrapped in a shroud and laid out at home. On the day of the burial, the community was summoned by the tolling of a bell. Friends and relatives often took turns carrying the coffin from the house of the deceased to the grave. The minister then gave a brief graveside speech.

After the burial, members of the funeral procession returned to the house of the deceased. Refreshments usually included cake and some sort of alcoholic beverage. At a well-attended funeral reception for Thomas Cobbett of Boston in 1685, the mourners managed to consume one entire barrel of wine and two of cider.

Toward the end of the 1600s, the custom of sending gloves to friends and acquaintances of the deceased as a gesture of invitation to the funeral took hold in New England.

Since ministers were invited to every funeral in their community, most acquired huge quantities of funeral gloves. The minister of Boston's North Meetinghouse "collected close to 3000 pair"[98] during the three decades he served as the church's pastor. Funeral rings were also commonly presented to mourners by the family of the deceased. Wealthy families gave away delicately crafted funeral rings inlaid with tiny, carved enamel skeletons, coffins, hourglasses, and other symbols of the fragility of human life.

The Puritan Legacy

By the final years of the seventeenth century, the influence of Puritanism in New England was fading. The region would never completely lose its distinctively Puritan character, but by 1700, Puritanism's hold over the social, religious, and political life of New England was increasingly challenged by other ideas and values.

An "Inordinate Affection to the World"

As the 1600s drew to a close, the communal ideal stressed by John Winthrop had lost much of its appeal for the people of New England. The compact, close-knit towns favored by the Puritan founding fathers were unraveling as more and more New Englanders chose to settle on isolated farms. Many factors contributed to the decline of the closely settled town in New England. The most important of these was probably the region's growing population. By the late 1600s, there was very little unclaimed farmland close to most towns. Consequently, newer residents had to go farther and farther from the center of town to reach farmland. Soon, people were building their houses far from the town center as well.

New England's growing economic prosperity further undercut the commitment of its inhabitants to traditional Puritan values. Older Puritan leaders like the Reverend Increase Mather decried what they saw as the materialism, selfish individualism, and "worldliness" of

their flocks. In a published address, Mather blasted the people of New England for their "inordinate affection to the world" and "insatiable desire after land and worldly accomodations." For far too many New Englanders, Mather complained, "farms and merchandising have been preferred before the things of God." The residents of the "city upon a hill" had forgotten their holy mission in America, he scolded. They were so focused on bettering

Reverend Increase Mather believed the growing economic prosperity of New England detached the Puritans from traditional values.

Puritans demonstrated a dedication to education that continues to influence U.S. school systems.

themselves financially, they were ignoring their spiritual health. If the New Englanders did not change their ways soon, Mather warned, "God will *change* either *you*, or your Government *ere* long."[99]

A New Charter

In 1691 Mather's prophecy came true when Massachusetts Bay, Puritan New England's largest and most influential colony, was forced to accept a new charter. Under the original charter, the colony had enjoyed almost complete autonomy. The new charter, which included Plymouth, made Massachusetts a royal colony and subjected its Puritan inhabitants to the unsympathetic control of the English monarch. Although Connecticut managed to hang on to its old charter, that colony too had to adhere strictly to the laws of England.

Increased royal control ended once and for all the Puritans' stranglehold on the spiri-

tual life of New England. Religious toleration—at least of other Protestant groups—was now required by law throughout New England. Anglicans, Baptists, Quakers, and other Protestants could erect their own churches and worship freely. Towns could no longer insist that a man be a member of a Puritan church in order to vote.

Our Puritan Inheritance

Yet if the Puritans' domination of New England had ended by 1700, many of their values and ideals have continued to influence Americans, right up to the present. Perhaps America's most important legacy from the Puritans is the emphasis placed on education in the United States. The first public schools in America were founded in New England by the Puritans. Today, funding of public school systems is typically the biggest item on the budgets of towns all over the United States.

The so-called Protestant work ethic is another aspect of America's Puritan inheritance. Like the Puritans, many present-day Americans place great emphasis on working hard and making every minute count. Also in common with the Puritans, many Americans believe that society has an obligation to help its less fortunate members. Just as the Puritans used public funds to assist those within their communities who were unable to support themselves or their families, Americans today are taxed to support public assistance programs such as Social Security, unemployment compensation, and public housing.

A final legacy from the Puritans is the American sense of mission. From the founding of the United States, Americans have viewed their nation as a sort of "city upon a hill." The United States was to serve as an example for the rest of the world to follow. It was to be a model for oppressed peoples everywhere of how a nation could prosper and thrive under a democratic form of government. Since Puritan times, Americans have assumed that they could change human society for the better, if only they worked together to attain their goals.

At the dawn of the eighteenth century, it might have seemed that the Puritans' holy experiment in the New World had failed. But in a very real sense, their "city upon a hill" still endures. In the emphasis which Americans place on education and hard work, in their assumption that society should take care of its least fortunate members, and in their sense of mission, it is evident that Puritan values influence the people of the United States even today, nearly four centuries after the Pilgrims first landed at Plymouth.

Notes

Chapter 1: Creating a New Society

1. John Winthrop, "A Model of Christian Charity . . .", reprinted in Alan Heimert and Andrew Delbanco, eds., *The Puritans in America: A Narrative Anthology*. Cambridge, MA: Harvard University Press, 1985, p. 91.
2. Winthrop, "A Model of Christian Charity," pp. 90–92.
3. Winthrop, "A Model of Christian Charity," p. 89.
4. Quoted in Virginia DeJohn Anderson, *New England's Generation: The Great Migration and the Formation of Society and Culture in the Seventeenth Century*. New York: Cambridge University Press, 1991, p. 161.
5. Quoted in Kenneth Lockridge, *A New England Town, the First Hundred Years: Dedham, Massachusetts, 1636–1736*. New York: Norton, 1970, p. 4.
6. Quoted in Richard L. Bushman, *From Puritan to Yankee: Character and the Social Order in Connecticut, 1690–1765*. Cambridge, MA: Harvard University Press, 1967, p. 13.
7. Quoted in Lockridge, *A New England Town*, p. 4.
8. Quoted in Stephen Foster, *Their Solitary Way: The Puritan Social Ethic in the First Century of Settlement in New England*. New Haven, CT: Yale University Press, 1971, p. 59.
9. Quoted in Carl Bridenbaugh, *Cities in the Wilderness: The First Century of Urban Life in America, 1625–1742*. New York: Knopf, 1955, pp. 63–64.
10. Quoted in Bridenbaugh, *Cities in the Wilderness*, p. 67.
11. Quoted in Foster, *Their Solitary Way*, p. 134.
12. Quoted in Bridenbaugh, *Cities in the Wilderness*, p. 82.
13. Quoted in Alice Morse Earle, *Colonial Dames and Good Wives*. Boston: Houghton Mifflin, 1895, p. 136.
14. Quoted in Earle, *Colonial Dames*, p. 96.
15. Quoted in Earle, *Colonial Dames*, p. 97.
16. Quoted in David D. Hall, *Worlds of Wonder; Days of Judgment: Popular Religious Belief in Early New England*. New York: Knopf, 1989, p. 180.
17. Samuel Sewall, *The Diary of Samuel Sewall, 1624–1729*, ed. M. Halsey Thomas, vol. 1. New York: Farrar, Strauss and Giroux, 1973, p. 509.

Chapter 2: Religion and the Supernatural

18. Quoted in Carl Bridenbaugh, *Early Americans*. New York: Oxford University Press, 1981, p. 258.
19. Quoted in Alice Morse Earle, *Child Life in Colonial Days*. 1899. Reprint, Stockbridge, MA: Berkshire House, 1993, p. 246.
20. Quoted in Francis J. Bremer, *The Puritan Experiment: New England Society from Bradford to Edwards*. New York: St. Martin's Press, 1976, p. 102.
21. Quoted in Bridenbaugh, *Early Americans*, p. 177.
22. Quoted in Hall, *Worlds of Wonder*, p. 169.

23. William Bradford, *Of Plymouth Planta-tion*, ed. Harvey Wish. New York: Capri-corn, 1962, pp. 12–13.

24. Quoted in Eugene Aubrey Stratton, *Ply-mouth Colony: Its History and People, 1620–1691*. Salt Lake City: Ancestry, 1986, pp. 95–96.

25. Quoted in Marilynne K. Roach, *In the Days of the Salem Witchcraft Trials*. Boston: Houghton Mifflin, 1996, p. 11.

26. Quoted in Heimert and Delbanco, *The Puritans in America*, p. 181.

27. Quoted in Emery Battis, *Saints and Sec-taries: Anne Hutchinson and the Antino-mian Controversy in the Massachusetts Bay Colony*. Chapel Hill: University of North Carolina Press, 1962, p. 208.

28. Quoted in John Demos, *Entertaining Satan: Witchcraft and the Culture of Early New England*. New York: Oxford University Press, 1982, p. 167.

29. Quoted in Demos, *Entertaining Satan*, p. 524.

30. Quoted in Demos, *Entertaining Satan*, p. 377.

31. Sewall, *The Diary of Samuel Sewall*, vol. 1, p. 12.

32. Quoted in Demos, *Entertaining Satan*, pp. 20, 167, 169.

33. Quoted in Richard Godbeer, *The Devil's Dominion: Magic and Religion in Early New England*. Cambridge, England: Cambridge University Press, 1992, p. 24.

34. Quoted in Hall, *Worlds of Wonder*, pp. 99–100.

35. Quoted in Demos, *Entertaining Satan*, pp. 138–39.

36. Quoted in Godbeer, *The Devil's Domin-ion*, p. 69.

Chapter 3: Working

37. Quoted in Bremer, *The Puritan Experi-ment*, p. 91.

38. Quoted in William Cronon, *Changes in the Land: Indians, Colonists, and the Ecology of New England*. New York: Hill and Wang, 1983, p. 134.

39. Quoted in Bridenbaugh, *Early Ameri-cans*, p. 92.

40. Quoted in Anderson, *New England's Generation*, p. 133.

41. Edward Johnson, *Johnson's Wonder-Working Providence, 1628–1651*, ed. J. Franklin Jameson. New York: Scribners, 1910, p. 209.

42. Quoted in George Francis Dow, *Every Day Life in the Massachusetts Bay Colony*. 1935. Reprint, New York: Dover, 1988, p. 149.

43. Quoted in Bridenbaugh, *Cities in the Wilderness*, p. 97.

44. Quoted in Bridenbaugh, *Cities in the Wilderness*, p. 38.

45. Johnson, *Johnson's Wonder-Working Providence*, p. 211.

46. Quoted in Anderson, *New England's Generation*, p. 145.

47. Quoted in Bridenbaugh, *Cities in the Wilderness*, p. 43.

48. Quoted in John Demos, *A Little Com-monwealth: Family Life in Plymouth Colony*. New York: Oxford University Press, p. 111.

49. Quoted in Clifford Lindsey Alderman, *Colonists for Sale: The Story of Inden-tured Servants in America*. New York: Macmillan, 1975, p. 134.

50. Quoted in Stratton, *Plymouth Colony*, p. 181.

51. Quoted in Bridenbaugh, *Cities in the Wilderness*, p. 200.

52. Quoted in Stratton, *Plymouth Colony*, p. 187.

53. Quoted in Demos, *A Little Common-wealth*, p. 72.

Chapter 4: At Home

54. Quoted in Edmund S. Morgan, *The Puritan Family: Religion and Domestic Relations in Seventeenth-Century New England*. Rev. ed., New York: Harper and Row, 1966, p. 149.
55. Quoted in Foster, *Their Solitary Way*, pp. 143–44.
56. Quoted in Stratton, *Plymouth Colony*, p. 94.
57. Quoted in Demos, *A Little Commonwealth*, p. 63.
58. Quoted in Bridenbaugh, *Cities in the Wilderness*, p. 277.
59. Quoted in Morgan, *The Puritan Family*, p. 46.
60. Quoted in Laurel Thatcher Ulrich, *Good Wives: Image and Reality in the Lives of Women in Northern New England, 1650–1750*. New York: Knopf, 1982, p. 41.
61. Quoted in Bridenbaugh, *Early Americans*, pp. 94–95.
62. Quoted in Dow, *Every Day Life*, p. 40.
63. Quoted in Earle, *Colonial Dames*, p. 284.
64. Quoted in Earle, *Colonial Dames*, p. 290.
65. Quoted in Bruce C. Daniels, *Puritans at Play: Leisure and Recreation in Colonial New England*. New York: St. Martin's, pp. 195–96.

Chapter 5: Growing Up Puritan

66. Quoted in Morgan, *The Puritan Family*, p. 92.
67. Quoted in Demos, *A Little Commonwealth*, pp. 134–35.
68. Quoted in Morgan, *The Puritan Family*, p. 103.
69. Quoted in Morgan, *The Puritan Family*, p. 148.
70. Sewall, *The Diary of Samuel Sewall*, vol. 1, p. 277.
71. Quoted in Benjamin W. Larabee, *Colonial Massachusetts: A History*. Millwood, NY: KTO Press, 1979, pp. 77–78.
72. Quoted in James Axtell, *The School Upon a Hill: Education and Society in Colonial New England*. New Haven, CT: Yale University Press, 1963, p. 171.
73. Quoted in Larabee, *Colonial Massachusetts*, p. 78.
74. Paul Leicester Ford, ed., *The New England Primer: A Reprint of the Earliest Known Edition*. New York: Dodd, Mead, 1897.
75. Quoted in Larabee, *Colonial Massachusetts*, p. 80.
76. Quoted in Axtell, *The School Upon a Hill*, p. 162.
77. Quoted in Bridenbough, *Cities in the Wilderness*, p. 127.
78. Quoted in Ulrich, *Good Wives*, p. 156.
79. Quoted in Daniels, *Puritans at Play*, p. 188.
80. Quoted in Ulrich, *Good Wives*, p. 74.
81. Sewall, *The Diary of Samuel Sewall*, vol. 1, p. 345.
82. Daniels, *Puritans at Play*, p. 94.

Chapter 6: Health and Medicine

83. Quoted in Dow, *Every Day Life*, p. 177.
84. Quoted in Bridenbaugh, *Cities in the Wilderness*, p. 88.
85. Quoted in Dow, *Every Day Life*, p. 175.
86. Quoted in Dow, *Every Day Life*, pp. 185, 187–88.
87. Quoted in Demos, *Entertaining Satan*, p. 81.
88. Quoted in Ulrich, *Good Wives*, p. 83.
89. Sewall, *The Diary of Samuel Sewall*, vol. 1, pp. 460–61.
90. Quoted in Bridenbaugh, *Cities in the Wilderness*, p. 87.
91. Quoted in Bridenbaugh, *Cities in the Wilderness*, p. 87.

92. Quoted in Hall, *Worlds of Wonder*, p. 204.
93. Cotton Mather, *The Diary of Cotton Mather*, vol. 1. Boston: Massachusetts Historical Society, 1912, p. 586.
94. Quoted in Bridenbaugh, *Cities in the Wilderness*, pp. 18, 85, 239.
95. Quoted in Dow, *Every Day Life*, p. 106.
96. Quoted in David Freeman Hawke, *Everyday Life in Early America*. New York: Harper & Row, 1988, p. 76.
97. Quoted in Hall, *Worlds of Wonder*, p. 54.
98. Quoted in David E. Stannard, *The Puritan Way of Death: A Study in Religion, Culture, and Social Change*. New York: Oxford University Press, 1977, p. 112.

Epilogue

99. Quoted in Larabee, *Colonial Massachusetts*, pp. 110–111.

For Further Reading

Clifford Lindsey Alderman, *Colonists for Sale: The Story of Indentured Servants in America*. New York: Macmillan, 1975. Describes the plight of indentured servants in the early American colonies.

Tracy Barrett, *Growing Up in Colonial America*. Brookfield, CT: Millbrook Press, 1995. Describes the day-to-day lives of children in Colonial America.

Beth Clark, *Anne Hutchinson*. Philadelphia: Chelsea House, 1999. Biography of a Puritan woman who dared to challenge her colony's male leadership.

Christopher Collier and James Lincoln Collier, *Pilgrims and Puritans, 1620–1676*. New York: Marshall Cavendish, 1998. Focuses on the political and institutional history of early New England.

Ruth Dean and Melissa Thomson, *Life in the American Colonies*. San Diego: Lucent Books, 1999. Topics include life in a colonial city, science and health, and crafts and professions.

Stuart A. Kallen, *The Salem Witch Trials*. San Diego: Lucent Books, 1999. Describes the background to the trials, different theories regarding the causes of the witch hysteria in late-seventeenth-century Salem, and the trials' aftermath.

Deborah Kent, *How We Lived in Colonial New England*. New York: Benchmark Books, 1999. An overview of day-to-day life in New England from its founding until 1776.

Lucille Recht Penner, *Eating the Plates: A Pilgrim Book of Food and Manners*. New York: Macmillan, 1991. Describes the diets and cooking techniques of the early New England colonists.

Marilynne K. Roach, *In the Days of the Salem Witchcraft Trials*. Boston: Houghton Mifflin, 1996. Places the Salem witchcraft trials within the context of everyday life in late-seventeenth-century New England.

Susan Neiburg Terkel, *Colonial American Medicine*. New York: Franklin Watts, 1993. Discusses physicians, common treatments, medical facilities, and other topics in early American medical history.

Works Consulted

Virginia DeJohn Anderson, *New England's Generation: The Great Migration and the Formation of Society and Culture in the Seventeenth Century*. New York: Cambridge University Press, 1991. Follows the lives of seven hundred Puritans who were among the earliest English colonists to settle in the Massachusetts Bay Colony.

James Axtell, *The School Upon a Hill: Education and Society in Colonial New England*. New Haven, CT: Yale University Press, 1963. A key work on education in early New England.

Emery Battis, *Saints and Sectaries: Anne Hutchinson and the Antinomian Controversy in the Massachusetts Bay Colony*. Chapel Hill: University of North Carolina Press, 1962. Details the life and beliefs of the controversial religious leader.

William Bradford, *Of Plymouth Plantation*. Ed. Harvey Wish. New York: Capricorn, 1962. A vital source for the history of early New England by the longtime governor of Plymouth Colony.

Francis J. Bremer, *The Puritan Experiment: New England Society from Bradford to Edwards*. New York: St. Martin's Press, 1976. Overview of New England society, with sections on theology, family life, education, science, and other topics.

Carl Bridenbaugh, *Cities in the Wilderness: The First Century of Urban Life in America, 1625–1742*. New York: Knopf, 1955. Detailed study of life in early America's cities and larger towns, including Boston.

———, *Early Americans*. New York: Oxford University Press, 1981. Collection of essays on early British America by one of the leading historians of colonial America.

Richard L. Bushman, *From Puritan to Yankee: Character and the Social Order in Connecticut, 1690–1765*. Cambridge, MA: Harvard University Press, 1967. Describes the decline of Puritanism in New England during the late-seventeenth and early-eighteenth centuries.

William Cronon, *Changes in the Land: Indians, Colonists, and the Ecology of New England*. New York: Hill and Wang, 1983. Examines the ways in which the Puritan colonists interacted with their New World environment.

Bruce C. Daniels, *Puritans at Play: Leisure and Recreation in Colonial New England*. New York: St. Martin's, 1995. Describes those leisure activities which the Puritans approved of, and those which they shunned.

John Demos, *Entertaining Satan: Witchcraft and the Culture of Early New England*. New York: Oxford University Press, 1982. Examines witchcraft and magic as a part of the day-to-day lives of Puritan New Englanders.

———, *A Little Commonwealth: Family Life in Plymouth Colony*. New York: Oxford University Press, 1970. Examines Puritan family life, child-rearing practices.

George Francis Dow, *Every Day Life in the Massachusetts Bay Colony*. 1935. Reprint, New York: Dover, 1988. Relies on probate records and other official documents to discuss housing, trade, crime, and other aspects of Puritan life.

Alice Morse Earle, *Child Life in Colonial Days*. 1899. Reprint, Stockbridge, MA: Berkshire House, 1993. A social history of colonial children, with particular attention to Puritan children.

————, *Colonial Dames and Good Wives*. Boston: Houghton Mifflin, 1895. A classic work on the role of women in colonial America.

Paul Leicester Ford, ed. *The New England Primer: A Reprint of the Earliest Known Edition*. New York: Dodd, Mead, 1897. New England's most popular primer, preceded by an informative introduction.

Stephen Foster, *Their Solitary Way: The Puritan Social Ethic in the First Century of Settlement in New England*. New Haven, CT: Yale University Press, 1971. Examines the hopes and inhibitions that shaped Puritan New Englanders' New World society and their day-to-day interactions.

Richard Godbeer, *The Devil's Dominion: Magic and Religion in Early New England*. Cambridge, England: Cambridge University Press, 1992. Describes the widespread practice of folk magic in New England in the face of strong opposition from the Puritan clergy.

David D. Hall, *Worlds of Wonder; Days of Judgment: Popular Religious Belief in Early New England*. New York: Knopf, 1989. Examines the spiritual beliefs of ordinary Puritans, including popular beliefs regarding magic and witchcraft.

David Freeman Hawke, *Everyday Life in Early America*. New York: Harper & Row, 1988. Details day-to-day life in the British American colonies.

Alan Heimert and Andrew Delbanco, eds., *The Puritans in America: A Narrative Anthology*. Cambridge, MA: Harvard University Press, 1985. Extensive collection of primary sources.

Edward Johnson, *Johnson's Wonder-Working Providence, 1628–1651*. Ed. J. Franklin Jameson. New York: Scribners, 1910. A contemporary narrative of early New England by a Puritan historian.

Jessica Kross, ed. *America Eras: The Colonial Era, 1600–1754*. New York: Gale Research, 1998. Includes chapters on business, education, science, and the arts.

Benjamin W. Larabee, *Colonial Massachusetts: A History*. Millwood, NY: KTO Press, 1979. A well-balanced account of the Massachusetts Bay Colony.

Kenneth Lockridge, *A New England Town, the First Hundred Years: Dedham, Massachusetts, 1636–1736*. New York: Norton, 1970. During the 1960s and 1970s, many local studies of colonial New England towns were published. Lockridge's study of Dedham is one of the best of these local "social histories."

Cotton Mather, *The Diary of Cotton Mather*. 2 vols. Boston: Massachusetts Historical Society, 1912. The diary of one of Puritan New England's most famous and influential ministers and writers.

Medicine in Colonial Massachusetts, 1620–1820. Colonial Society of Massachusetts, Publications, LVII. Boston: Colonial Society of Massachusetts, 1980. A collection of essays on the practice of medicine in early Massachusetts.

Edmund S. Morgan, *The Puritan Family: Religion and Domestic Relations in Seventeenth-Century New England*. Rev. ed. New York: Harper and Row, 1966. Study of Puritan family life by one of America's most respected historians.

Samuel Sewall, *The Diary of Samuel Sewall, 1674–1729*. Ed. M. Halsey Thomas. 2 vols. New York: Farrar, Straus and

Giroux, 1973. Diary of the prominent Puritan judge and merchant.

David E. Stannard, *The Puritan Way of Death: A Study in Religion, Culture, and Social Change*. New York: Oxford University Press, 1977. Discusses Puritan attitudes toward death and Puritan funeral practices.

Eugene Aubrey Stratton, *Plymouth Colony: Its History and People, 1620–1691*. Salt Lake City: Ancestry, 1986. Relies heavily on primary source material to allow the Pilgrims to tell their story in their own words.

Laurel Thatcher Ulrich, *Good Wives: Image and Reality in the Lives of Women in Northern New England, 1650–1750*. New York: Knopf, 1982. Provides fascinating details about the day-to-day lives of Puritan women.

Index

Account of Two Voyages, An (Josselyn), 90
agriculture
    boys and, 67–68
    diet and, 87–89
    farms, 38–41, 92
    fast days and, 27
    kitchen gardens, 15
ale, 89–90
Algonquians, 14
anesthesia, 82
Anglican Communion, 9
apothecaries, 82
apprenticeship, 21, 74–75, 82
architecture
    of houses, 55–59
    of meetinghouses, 24–25
    of schoolhouses, 69–70
armies, 16
artisans, 47–48, 74–75
Axtell, James, 74

bartering, 40
bathing, 86
Battis, Emery, 30
bedsteads, 59–60
beer, 78
"bees," 77–78
"Before the Birth of One of Her Children" (Bradstreet), 84
behavior
    of children, 52, 67
    in church, 29
    recreation and, 75–76
    on Sabbath, 20
    see also punishment
berrying, 78
beverages, 78, 89–90
blacksmiths, 47–48
blasphemy, 20
Boston, Massachusetts
    firefighting in, 19
    garbage disposal in, 87

as port town, 41
Boylston, Zabiel, 84
boys
    education of, 72
    jobs of, 67–68
    recreation for, 78
    see also children
Bradford, William, 28
Bradstreet, Anne Dudley, 46, 84
breadmaking, 44
bucket brigade, 18–19
Bulkley, John, 17

Calvin, John, 9, 10
candles, 57
carpenters, 47
Catholicism, 9, 24, 27–28
"chairman of the board," 63
charity, 19, 94
charms, 36
chests, 59
childbirth, 84–85
children
    chores for, 67–69, 72
    clothing for, 66
    furniture for, 61–62
    rearing of, 52, 67
    recreation for, 75
    as servants, 50–51
    sinfulness and, 67
    work of, 67–69
    see also boys; girls
Christmas, 27–28
church officials, 26, 28–29
    see also ministers
cider, 89–90
"city upon a hill"
    as ideal, 12
    role of family and, 67
    United States as, 94
cleanliness, 86–87
cloth, 44

clothing, 63–64
Connecticut, 11, 93
constables, 17
cooking, 63, 86
coopers, 47
Corey, Giles, 34
corn, 88–89
cornhusking, 77–78
corporal punishment, 70–71, 75
courting, 52–53
cradles, 62
crime, 19–20

dancing, 76
Day of Doom, The (Wigglesworth), 76
death, 90–91
decor, 57–58
Dedham, Massachusetts, 15, 17
diet, 87–89
discipline, 67, 70–71, 75
    see also behavior; punishment
disease, 84–86
    see also hygiene; medicine
dishes, 63, 86
dissenters, religious, 29–32
doctors, 79–82
    see also medicine
domestic work, 42–46, 68–69
Dorchester, Massachusetts, 16
Downing, Mary, 65
dress code, 64, 74
ducking chairs, 22
"dugouts," 55–56
dye, 63
dysentery, 86

eating, 63, 86
economy, 92
Edmonds, Anna, 83

education, 69–75, 93
  of doctors, 79
  of lawyers, 21
  of ministers, 28
  of surgeons, 82
  see also schools
"Elect," 10, 16
Elementary Spelling Book
  (Webster), 71
emigration, 10–11
Endecott, Zerobabel, 81–82
England, 12–13, 93
evil, good vs., 32–33
executions, 22–23, 31–32

farms. *See* agriculture
fast days, 26–27, 85
fire
  construction of fireplaces,
    58–59
  firefighting, 18–19
  importance of, 43–44
fishing, 40–41, 74, 76
fortune telling, 36
Foster, Stephen, 64
funerals, 90–91
furniture, 59–64

Galen, 80
gambling, 76
garbage, 86–87
gardens, 15
  see also agriculture
Gifford, George F., 90
girdling, 38
girls
  domestic work for, 68–69
  education of, 72
  recreation for, 78
  see also children
gloves, 90–91
good vs. evil, 32–33
government, 16–17
greens, 15
gristmills, 15–16

hairstyles, 74
harrows, 39

Harvard University, 28, 72–74
health, 84–90
  see also medicine
heat, 24–25, 58–59, 69–70
Henry VIII, King, 9
Henseley, Jeannine, 46
Higginson, John, 42
hornbooks, 71–72
houses, 55–59
housewives, 42–46, 68–69
Hubbard, William, 17, 40
Hull, John, 85
humors, 80
hunting, 76
Hutchinson, Anne, 30–31
hygiene, 86–87

"idle poor," 19
incantations, 36
indentured servants, 48–50
infection, 82
  see also medicine
inoculation, 84, 85

jails, 23
Johnson, Edward, 40, 44, 88
Josselyn, John, 90
judicial system, 19–23, 33–35

Knopp, Nicholas, 79

laborers, 48–51
land grants, 13–15
Lechford, Thomas, 25–26
leeches, 80–81
legal system, 19–23, 33–35
life span, 79
lighting, 57
"liners," 26
livestock, 40, 87, 88
Luther, Martin, 9
luxury trades, 48

magic. *See* witchcraft
Maine, 11
marriage, 52–55
Massachusetts Bay Colony, 9,
  11

clothing law, 64
fast days in, 27
marriage law, 52
schools of, 69, 72
  *see also individual town and
    city names*
Massachusetts General Court,
  52, 69, 72
Mather, Cotton, 17, 22–23, 59
  on clothing, 65, 74
  on disciplining children, 67
  on family life, 52
  on mental illness, 86
  smallpox inoculation and, ex-
    periment of, 84, 85
  on witchcraft, 36–37
Mather, Increase, 36, 37, 92
mattresses, 60
Mayflower, 8
meat, 88
medicine, 82
  bleeding, 80–81
  doctors, shortage of, 79–80
  health concerns, 84–90
  tobacco as, 90
*Medicine in Colonial Massa-
  chusetts* (Gifford), 90
meetinghouses, 15, 24–25
men
  clothing for, 65–66
  traditional roles of, 44–46
mental illness, 85–86
merchants, 41–42
Metacomet, Chief, 14
midwives, 84–85
militias, 16, 78
ministers, 28–29
  education of, 73
  medical advice of, 79–80
  see also individual names
morality, 12
  family and, 52, 67
  lessons of, 77
mortality rates, infant, 79
music, 26

Native Americans, 14, 78
New England Primer, 71–72

New Hampshire, 11
Newman, Samuel, 17
Newport, Rhode Island, 41, 86–87
nutrition, 87–89

"Old Deluder Law," 69, 72
Oliver, Mary, 30–31

Paddy, William, 59–60
paganism, 28
Parris, Samuel, 29
periwigs, 74
Perkins, William, 38
persecution, 10–11
pets, 25
Philip, King, 14
pigs, 87, 88
Pilgrims, 8
pillories, 21–22
pintadoes (quilts), 60
Planters Plea, The (White), 40
plows, 39
Plymouth Colony, 8, 11
    Christmas in, 28
    marriage law of, 52
    Massachusetts, combined with, 93
portent, 33
primers, 71–72
prisons, 23
privacy, 13, 57, 86
prophecy. *See* portent
Protestant Reformation, 9
Protestant work ethic, 94
public assistance, 19, 94
"puddin' head," 66
pumpkins, 88
punishment
    for blasphemy, 20
    for crimes, 21–23
    portent and, 33
    of Quakers, 31–32
    for witchcraft, 33–35
    see also discipline
purging, 80–81
Puritanism
    church officials, 26, 28–29

decline of, 92–94
defined, 8
development of, 9–10
meetinghouses, 15, 24–25
see also ministers; religious beliefs; social structure

Quakers, 31–32
quilts, 60

"raisings," 77
reading, 69, 76–77
recreation, 74–76
Reformation, 9
religious beliefs
    blasphemy, 20
    challenging Puritan teachings, 29–32
    child rearing and, 67
    Christmas, 27–28
    church services, 25–27
    conversion, 14
    good vs. evil, 32–33
    literature about, 76–77
    persecution and, 10–11
    salvation, 10, 16, 67
Religious Society of Friends, 31–32
repentance, 27
Rhode Island, 11, 41, 69, 86–87
rings, 91
Robinson, John, 67
"room and board," 63
rushlights, 57

Sabbath, 20, 25–26
Saints and Sectaries: Anne Hutchinson and the Antinomian Controversy in the Massachusetts Bay Colony (Battis), 30
Salem, Massachusetts, 34, 41
    see also witchcraft
Saltonstall, Elizabeth, 75
salvation, 10, 16, 67
sanitation, 86–87
Satan, 32–33, 69, 85

schools
    buildings for, 69–70
    college, 72–74
    dame, 69
    funding for, 69, 93
    grammar, 72
    schoolmasters, 70–71
    see also education
School Upon a Hill: Education and Society in Colonial New England, The (Axtell), 74
selectmen, 16
servants, 47–51
settles, 59
Sewall, Betty (daughter), 76
Sewall, Samuel, 22–23
    on childbirth customs, 85
    on medicine, 82
    on weddings, 54
silversmiths, 48
slavery, 50
smallpox, 84, 85
smoking, 90
soap, 86
socializing, 78
social structure, 11
    clothing and, 64
    hierarchy of, 12
    leadership and, 17
spelling, 71
spinning thread, 44
spirit world, 32–33
sports, 76
stocks, 21–22
stone walls, 38
stools, 62
superstition, 32–33, 36–37
surgery, 82

tables, 63
taxes
    to fund schools, 69, 93
    to pay minister, 28–29
Tenth Muse, Lately Sprung Up in America, The (Bradstreet), 46
Thanksgiving, 26–27

Their Solitary Way: The Puritan Social Ethic in the First Century of Settlement in New England (Foster), 64
tithingmen, 29
Tituba, 34
tobacco, 90
tools, 38–39
towns, 15–16
trading, 40
trees, 38, 40
trenchers, 63

utensils, 63, 86

Virginia, 11
voting, 16, 93

warming pans, 60

watchmen, 17–18
wealth, distribution of, 12, 14
    attitudes toward poor, 19
    mercantile elite, 42
weaving, 44
Webster, Noah, 71
weddings, 53–54
whispering sticks, 71
White, John, 40
Wigglesworth, Michael, 55–56, 76, 79–80
Williams, Roger, 30, 89
Winthrop, John, 9, 11
    Anne Hutchinson and, 30
    "city upon a hill" sermon, 12
witchcraft, 33–37
women
    clothing for, 64–65
    domestic work of, 42–46

medicine practiced by, 83–85
nontraditional jobs of, 46–47
prohibited from attending college, 73
rights of, 55
role of, in church life, 30
as teachers, 70
traditional roles of, 44–46
unmarried, 47
voting regulations and, 16
Woodbridge, John, 46
work ethic, 94
Works of Anne Bradstreet, The (Henseley), 46
"worthy poor," 19
writing, 71

yokes, 71

Picture Credits

About the Author

Louise Chipley Slavicek received her master's degree in American history from the University of Connecticut. She has written many articles on historical subjects for both scholarly journals and children's magazines. She lives in Ohio with her husband, Jim, a research biologist, and her children, Krista and Nathan.